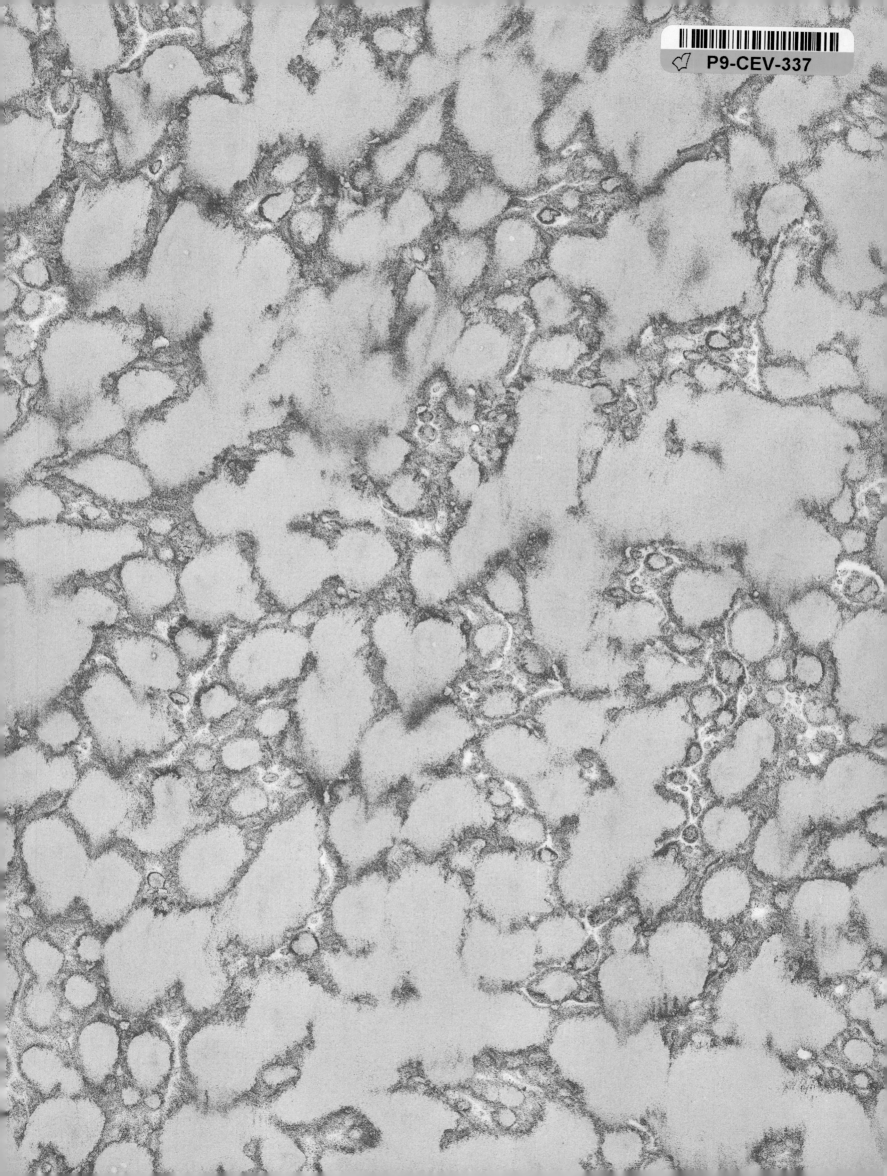

First published in the United States of America in 1993 by
RIZZOLI INTERNATIONAL PUBLICATIONS, INC.
300 Park Avenue South, New York, NY 10010

Copyright © Editions Didier Millet

Library of Congress Cataloging-in-Publication Data

Nantet, Bernard.
Cheeses of the World: an illustated guide for gourmets / by Bernard Nantet.
p. cm.
Includes table of cheeses and index
ISBN 0-8478-1599-4
1. Cheese. 2. Cheese-Varieties. 3. Cheese-History. 4. Cookery
(Cheese) I. Title
SF271.N34   1992
641.3'73—dc20
92-9392
CIP

EDITORIAL COORDINATION: FRANÇOISE BOTKINE
ADDITIONAL TEXT AND RESEARCH: CORINNE HEWLETT
TRANSLATION FROM THE FRENCH: CLIO MITCHELL, ROB JAMIESON AND DANIEL WHEELER
PICTURE RESEARCH: MAUD FISHER-OSOSTOWICZ, MARYSE HUBERT, SHONA WOOD

Printed and bound in Italy by Editoriale Libraria

CHEESES
OF THE WORLD

■ TEXT ■

BERNARD NANTET

PATRICK RANCE

FRANÇOISE BOTKINE

NINETTE LYON

JEAN CLAUDE RIBAUT

■ DESIGN ■

LOUISE BRODY

■ PHOTOGRAPHS ■

JEAN-PIERRE DIETERLEN

RIZZOLI
NEW YORK

C O N T

E N T S

FOREWORD

L et me put cheese into world perspective: two fifths of humanity eat no cheese. Over most of the Far East and South-East Asia, bovines provide haulage power and meat but are milked only by their young. In India and the Himalayas butter made from yak's and buffalo's milk is clarified to *ghi* for religious, culinary and medicinal uses; but cheese depends on European initiative or influence. I have enjoyed Nepalese yak and buffalo cheese made under Swiss tutelage. Further north the Mongols ferment mare's milk into *kumiss*. Over the rest of the world more ewes are milked than cows, and a host of goats. These mountain species evolved spectacularly, sheep not always easily distinguishable from goats. They were widely domesticated before history began. The poor Cyclops, gate-crashed, blinded and robbed by Odysseus, was a shepherd and cheese-maker. Later, 8th-century BC Greeks colonised distant shores, whence Sicily's Pecorino, its milk stirred with a fig branch to reinforce the animal rennet. Pyrenean Basques claim to have been making Ardi-Gasna from ewe's milk "forever". "Forever" is probably as true of Armenian and Georgian shepherds in the Trans-Caucasus and their sheep's cheese. Perhaps it might even have been on the Ark, since the Georgians allege their descent from Noah. The Turks spread ewe's milk cheeses and fermented milk from The Orient and Arabia as far as Vienna. They had already taken sheep dairy across North Africa into Iberia. Thence the *conquistadores* took it to South America, where llamas had been milked, but sheep and cheese were still unknown.

The northern Old World has seen faster changes. Except in France, sheep dairy receded towards the end of the medieval era. Monastic enterprise, which had initiated and organised much cheese dairy, weakened at the Reformation. Hard and semi-hard cow's milk cheeses, mainstay of the Netherlands, Britain, Alpine regions and the Pyrenees, were, and are, often made in village cooperatives. They vary from valley to valley. English Cheddar dominated New World cheese-making. In Europe most farms made cheese, developing hundreds of varieties in France, and dozens in Britain (lost after war broke out in 1939).

Modern industrial cheese results from the demand for quantity above quality, imposed by wartime governments and postwar supermarkets. Multi-species grassland was ploughed up, re-seeded with one or two-species leys, and chemically fertilised. Milk from Friesian cows, lower in fat and protein, supplanted the milk of Normandes, Vosgiennes, Salers, Shorthorns, Ayrshires and Gloucesters, breeds associated with traditional cheeses. Machines replaced cheese-makers. Cheeses became block-shaped, plastic-sealed and chilled, or made from extruded curd with an artificial thick white

coating. These replaced patiently perfected raw-milk cheeses, which could breathe and mature healthily in natural coats while accruing an ever-increasing flavour and aroma. In the 1970s cheese lovers rebelled. A new wave of traditional cheese-makers counter-attacked in France, Britain, North America and the Antipodes. In the Old World some makers revived venerable traditional cheeses, while some developed new ones; until European Community Milk Quotas cut the good with the bad and strangled small producers with unscientifically-based panic regulations.

In the New World, cheese-makers introduced Old World cheeses and also established native originals. The traditional and new artisanal cheeses are in a different class of food from modern industrial products. The latter are tailored to mass-trade convenience, rather than to customers' requirements. The difference, and the lessons learned, should be studied in those parts of the world where mistakes made in the West can still be avoided. They begin literally at grass-roots level.

Industrial cheese-makers (with some French exceptions) disregard healthy tradition in farming and dairy. New-wave and surviving traditional cheese-making farmers constantly repay to the soil organically the goodness used up by grazing beasts and haymaking. Their permanent grassland can harbour fifty or more native plant-species, ensuring disease-resistance, and a longer productivity as the various species follow each other throughout the season. As with vines and wine, the older the pastures, the richer the cheese in bouquet and flavour. Higher yield is stimulated by close-grazing: not only by manure and the benefits of grazers' feet to the tilth, but by growth-stimulant in their saliva as they tackle the first three inches of plant shoots. This can raise yields by one seventh, and gives the animal the most nourishing part of the plant.

There are two basic reasons for cheese-makers to keep to tradition on the farm. Firstly, multi-species permanent pastures yield milk for vintage cheese; their variety is good for the animals, and the animals love it. A senior agricultural botanist told me: "The one- and two-species ley is the bovine equivalent of junk food". Secondly, the whole structure of local character, aroma and flavour, and healthy bacterial balance in milk and cheese, is undermined by chemical fertilisers and sprays: "Soils have an enormous influence on pastures, but it has been largely obliterated by modern grassland management". This verdict was given me by the world's greatest expert on soil fertility, Dr. George Cooke. Land so mismanaged cannot sustain the pasture we need. Chemicals destroy much of the bacterial, insect and worm population that nourish and aerate the soil, which is thus affected. This discourages deep root-penetration of legumes (such as lucerne and clovers), whose rhyzomes naturally entrap nitrogen for themselves and plant neighbours.

Disproportionate growth of tall species shades out shorter plants, including clovers. The chemically-achieved extra weight of grass is of an insipid character.

Organic farming cherishes soil-life, enriches the earth and perpetuates the healthy balance and variety of local species. Soil bacteria and minerals are transmitted via the plant-oils into the body-fat and mammary glands of the grazing animal along with the plant's aromatic esters. Thence they pass with the milk fat into the cheese, provided the milk is used raw, and the fat is not removed.

Heat treatment of any kind diminishes character. Pasteurisation kills 99% of bacteria and nullifies the vital aromatic esters. This can be costly to health as well as to palatability. Milk's natural bacteria ensure high acidity in properly-made raw-milk cheese, suppressing the toxic potential of *Staphylococcus aureus*, common in milk. They also suppress *Listeria monocytogenes*. Cheese-makers should observe acidity measurements laid down for the stages of making (final pH of 5 or below is safe; 5.5 or above is dangerous; pH perversely measures alkalinity, so high acidity is low pH.) Listeria can survive pasteurisation and multiply in the cheese (or penetrate it from outside), if its acidity is too low. Pasteurisation has also killed the beneficent bacteria needed to defeat listeria, which thrives in low temperatures where competitive bacteria cannot survive. This explains its presence in many cold-counter mass-produced soft cheeses. Until the post-war excesses of chemical farming and silage-making, listeria was scarcely heard of. There is evidence that in soil undisturbed by chemicals, the natural bacterial balance will exclude listeria, as it does in healthy raw milk cheese. A French cheese *Appellation* authority has found no listeria in milk samples from its numerous organic farms in over a year since tests began.

Dr. J G Davis, a farm and factory-based cheese-maker, speaks from the inside as a chemist and bacteriologist: "The commonest danger in pasteurising is the assumption... that it will make dirty milk clean and eliminate all troubles of bacteriological origin. But a well-made (unpasteurised) cheese is virtually never the cause of food poisoning".

These are the foundations of quality and natural local variety in cheese: organically-farmed permanent grassland grazed by traditional dairy breeds (in winter, hay, not silage as food); strict hygiene in milking-parlour and dairy (exclusion of any milk given by cows under antibiotics or suspected of mastitis); traditional cheese-making methods using raw milk, and paying constant attention to acidity. Dr. Davis recommends locally-made starters, or for "the best cheese of all... natural souring of the milk with no starter". This, I can promise you from rich experience, is the path to cheeses of incomparable aroma, flavour and succulence.   ■ PATRICK RANCE

Le signore pasando
per la per la piasa ve denbro
le putane à filar ti conbo
fà catino t'impo

Vna filara in pasando dice
an te putane filou
subito la fato risposta le sigore
àno derato, il pane et bisonia filare
ce, volemo, maniar

Lo filo meglio con ma al core es como io filto non è ancora
copano il fuso io piango del mio marito ha mi à pinciato
delle sue nhone che sta bene io son agiusata cha dui
speciario à pistar il povano io sto allegrismente
et sapete quello che mi da al giorno da maghare ni giono
mi da vn oncia di pane o vn oncia di acqua se
sapesi che il sta alegro non è mai perso questi
grani son vn porcho à tanto tempo cha io frauatio
non è ancora potuto avensarmi da corprare vn di
Maniga dua uesnio lo sta milan se ouste da bisogno
di gliasuini vn gran signere

CHEESE AND CIVILISATION

Although the Near East first gave cheese to the world, it was in the temperate climates of Europe that the delicacy really flourished, helped above all by medieval monastic orders, who perfected the production methods of a number of great cheeses. The simultaneous rise of the town and its markets enabled cheeses from even the remotest regions to become well-known far beyond their places of origin. Other parts of the world meanwhile were not blessed by such favourable climatic conditions: milk-derivatives were spoiled or dried out by the heat in Africa, and vulnerable to the monsoon climate in India and South-East Asia. Where land might have been suited to stock-rearing in China and Japan, it was put under rice cultivation instead.

For hundreds of thousands of years, hunting and gathering were the only forms of human subsistence. Sufficient food and clothing was provided by the capture of large mammals. The bones of the latter also served to make tools that were finer and more accurate than stone implements. The vital importance of hunting, probably as much for religious and magical reasons as for sustenance, is eloquently testified by the magnificent cave-paintings of Spain, south-west France and the Ahaggar Mountains in the Sahara.

With the advent of the herding of sheep, goats, cattle and reindeer, milk, which had been a rare treat, entered into daily use. The actual "invention" of cheese was probably a happy accident resulting from the discovery of the curd formed by milk that had been left exposed to the sun or close to the fire for a few hours. The history of cheese is therefore indissolubly linked with that of the domestication of animals and stock-rearing.

DOMESTICATION

In the mesolithic age, while the ice was still retreating from Europe, hunters living in the relatively temperate climate of the Near East traded their hunting-spears for shepherds' crooks and set about mastering the animals and plants of the natural world. This process was taking place about 10,000 years before the present era. The first animal to be domesticated by the nomads was the dog, which helped them with the hunting. Next, in about 8000 BC, came the sheep, or to be more precise, the Iranian mouflon. This was followed shortly by the goat, which was first tamed in the same region.

Most Near Eastern archaeological sites dating from the 7th millenium BC reveal traces of domesticated sheep and goats, which also featured in archaic mythologies as the companions or wetnurses of the gods. Later, in about 6500 BC, came the domestication of pigs and, at around 5000 BC,

The age-old image of a shepherd carrying a lamb across his shoulders; in his hand, a basket filled with cheeses. A scene of everyday life from a Byzantine mosaic of the 6th-7th century. Courtyard floor mosaic. *Mosaics Museum, Topkapi Palace, Istanbul.* PRECEDING PAGES: an anonymous late 15th-century fresco, depicting "Vendors of cheese and savouries", *Issogne Castle, Val d'Aoste.*

small cattle. Buffalo were grouped into herds in Asia in about 3000 BC. So it was that the former hunter-gatherer gradually turned into a producer, raising animals for meat and milk, harvesting cereals, and ensuring the reproductive cycles of both. With this development, civilisation was born.

THE DISCOVERY OF POTTERY

To talk of civilisation is inevitably to invoke cooking, "that slow process of elaboration which transforms an unappealing raw substance into a delicacy" (Georges Pérec). What made this process possible was the fundamental technological discovery of pottery, or baked earth. Previously, grilling had been the only way of preparing food. Pottery made it possible to cook meats and cereals together, as well as to add other ingredients, such as herbs and wild roots. The advent of cheese and the creation of diverse varieties went hand in hand with this quest for taste and flavour. By the 5th millenium BC therefore, everything was set for the production of milk and cheese to begin. The first domesticated sheep and goats appeared in Italy, southern France and North Africa in this period. The design of the decorated ceramics used by the stockbreeders indicates that they were used for straining whey.

Indisputable evidence of cheese-making in Europe, going back as far as 2800 BC, is revealed in the remains of vessels with holes punched in them, clearly serving to drain curds. These *faisselles*, or moulds, made out of terracotta or rushes, offer a useful insight into this antique industry. They have been found in Lagozza in Italy (near Varese in Lombardy), and also in Chassey in France (Burgundy). This type of soft white cheese mould is still used today, particularly in the farmhouse production of ordinary cheeses. A basketwork *faisselle* fitted with a cloth base to form a strainer, has also been found among other basketwork objects on the marshy shores of Lake Neufchâtel in Switzerland.

GOATS, SHEEP AND CATTLE

The peoples of the Danube valley and the Balkans were responsible for introducing the cow into Europe, in the 4th millenium BC. These populations kept a very varied stock including sheep, goats, pigs and cattle. Ever since then, bovines have remained more numerous in the north and caprines more widespread in the south. The former have been given all the rich plains, the lush valleys with their regular rainfall, and the sunny alpine pastures. Sheep and goats have had to make do with all the bleak and hostile lands: the gullied and eroded regions, the Mediterranean countries with their miserable grass, and the hard, rocky, wet and wind-lashed terrains of Ireland and the North Sea islands.

Fresco by J Giacomo (15th century) representing a pastoral scene with cows and sheep. San Antonio di Ranverso, Abbazia.

Neolithic pottery cheese moulds from Chassey (Burgundy, France). *Rolin Museum, Autun.* OPPOSITE: a mosaic depicting a Roman banquet, *circa* 200-220 AD, and confirming the existence of stock-rearing in North Africa in this period. *Pardo Palace, Tunisia.*

MYTHOLOGIES

In the earliest mythologies, the prevalence of female milk-bearing figures – cows, goats and sheep – testifies to the importance of such animals. Shepherds were even invested with superhuman powers. The cult of great fertility symbols is linked to the consumption of dairy products: milk and cheese are the legendary foods of gods and heroes. Myths common to the ancient Nordic religions evoke the chaos which originally reigned over the world in the following way: "There was no ground then. No lakes, no salty waves, no earth facing the sky above. It was a bottomless abyss, with no grass anywhere". In the north, there were mountains of ice all shrouded in mist, while the south burned red with the flames of an eternal fire. From the encounter of these two the giant Ymir was born, and out of the melting ice came the cow, Audumla. The latter's milk revived the strength of the giant, who then gave birth to two more giants, one male, one female. They in turn gave birth to a daughter, Bestla. Audumla also created the first man, by licking and thawing a rock covered in frost. This Nordic Adam married Bestla, the giants' daughter, and the fruits of their union were the three great gods of the Scandinavian pantheon: Odin, Ve and Vili.

SUMERIA

The Sumerians of the 3rd millenium BC, who invented writing, believed that Enlil, the second god of their pantheon and lord of the earth, was the "shepherd who presides over destinies". Legend has it that as a result of the development of writing and stock-rearing, "the land became vast, men multiplied there and the country was saturated as by livestock". Enlil, a jealous and tetchy god, decided to punish man for his presumptuousness. He caused a great flood and told his favourite, Ziusuddu, to gather one pair of every animal in creation onto a great boat. Seven days later Ziusuddu reached dry land and "sacrificed an ox and immolated a sheep" by way of a thankyou to the gods.

BABYLON

The importance of milk and its derivatives also appears in the fertility cults of the Babylonians, who conquered and inherited Sumerian culture. A bas-relief on the pediment of a temple in Ur (2500 BC) depicts the rearing of livestock, including cowsheds, the milking of cows, and butter-making, according to a method still used until recently between the Tigris and the Euphrates. The milk was poured into a large earthenware jar and stirred, rather like churning, by a man who held the jar firm between his legs. The milk was then filtered to separate out the lumps of butter, which were put into another pot. But Babylonian civilisation has left us some much more detailed evidence. In this city of debauchery, condemned to destruction by the biblical prophets, people ate, drank and made merry. The various

dishes in a royal feast have been recorded in cuneiform on clay tablets. Meats of all kinds (goat, horse, donkey, beef and mutton), dairy products, including *tommes,* spiced cheeses and soft cheese, and a number of fruits and honeys for making patisseries, all featured. Cheese-making was highly developed; there were no fewer than twenty different names for soft cheeses alone.

By about the 3rd millenium BC, nomadism was no more than a dim and distant memory in the minds of settled men. Granaries for storing the crop and enclosures for protecting the herds were by then the norm. Such riches had to be defended against the attacks of neighbouring peoples, and patriarchy emerged triumphant. The cult of the moon and its cycles, linked to reproductive cycles, was superseded by adoration of the sun and his chariot in popular belief. The cow, the ewe and the she-goat were no longer venerated, replaced by the males who impregnated them: the bull was divinised by agricultural peoples from the Near East, the ram by Mesopotamian shepherds and the he-goat in ancient Greece.

THE HEBREWS

The Eternal fed his chosen people on "honey out of the rocks [...] the butter of kine, and milk of sheep, with fat of lambs, and rams of the breed of Bashan, and goats, with the fat of kidneys of wheat; and [...] the pure blood of the grape" *(Deuteronomy, 31:14).* But when they entered into "the land of milk and honey" (an image of paradise that was already current in Sumeria), these nomadic shepherds with their herds of goats found rich pastures suited to agriculture and cattle-rearing. Their life became easier and the consequences are well-known: they forgot their promise and gave themselves up to the cult of the Golden Calf, which was flourishing all over the Near East and the Mediterranean region in this period. In the Bible, cheese is the food of heroes. It was while the frail young shepherd David was delivering cheese to his brothers, to sustain them in their combat with the Philistines, that

A banquet and parade of offerings, all of which are the products of stock-raising or agriculture, in Mesopotamia, circa 2500 BC. Ur tomb, *British Museum, London.* BELOW: the bull who sired their herds enabled lazy farmers to live such an easy, want-free life that they forgot all they owed to their Creator and fell to worshipping the Golden Calf.

he accepted the giant Goliath's challenge and felled him, armed with only a simple sling. When he became a father, David decreed that his son Solomon should be given "goat's milk in abundance for his food", perhaps in memory of his own victory.

GREECE

Greek mythology accords a privileged place to the goat, and her milk and cheese. The traces of an archaic cult of milk-giving animals can be seen in Amalthea, the goat who saved Zeus. Cronos, the master of time, had vowed that his son, Zeus, must die. Fortunately, Amalthea nourished the infant and brought him up secretly to keep him safe from Cronos. One day the child who was to become the lord of thunder and of all the gods, accidentally broke one of the goat's horns while playing. To console her, he promised that it would miraculously be filled with all the fruits she could wish for: that is, that it would become the horn of plenty.

During the seige of Troy, the combatants were able to recover from their trials and struggles thanks to the drink served to them by Hecamede, "the beautiful captive". She gave them "wine and goat's cheese that she herself had crumbled on a bronze grater, with the finest white flour in a cup of bronze with four handles, adorned with golden studs". (*Iliad*, book XI).

In the course of his many adventures, Ulysses, the hero of the *Odyssey*, came ashore on the island inhabited by Polyphemus, the terrifying Cyclops. It is often forgotten that this grotesque giant, who proceeded to imprison Ulysses and his companions in his cave, was also a shepherd. Homer's text describes a shepherd's life and the way the milk was used in detail: "There it was that our human monster had his shelter [...] We entered into the cavern and looked around it: racks laden with cheeses, lambs and kid goats in crowded pens – one stall for every age, the older here, the younger there, and the new-born further along – metal pots, all filled with milk, earthenware vessels, buckets used for milking". The Cyclops, who had returned to the cave where his animals and the ship-wrecked Greeks were penned in, closed it up with a boulder and set out to "milk the whole of his bleating flock of sheep and goats one after another, then, leaving a little one under the udder of each, he turned half of his white milk to a curd, which he strained and placed in his rush basket, but he kept the rest of his pots to drink with his supper." (*Odyssey*, book IX). It may be noted that the brutish Polyphemus had a highly developed sense of pastoral economy. Centuries of rearing had taught men to make the most of their herds, so that they took the first of the milk, which is the thinnest, and left the richest part for the baby animals to suckle. The shepherd made some cheese, keeping back some of the fresh milk for his own consumption.

The goat Amalthea nursing Zeus. Sculpture by Bernini (17th century). *Borghese Gallery, Rome.*

The Mosclophoros. The shepherd, who was a figure of legend, or a god, frequently appears with a sheep on his shoulders in the art of Ancient Greece. OPPOSITE: marble sculpture, *Acropolis Museum, Athens.*

ROME

When the Romans' dominion extended across the world, goat's and sheep's cheese formed the daily diet of the commoners: the peasants, villagers and slaves. And yet Romulus and Remus, the founders of Rome, were nourished on wolf's milk, after having been thrown into the Tiber by a jealous uncle. The Romans considered goat's milk as the most nourishing and easily digestible milk, and doctors recommended it warmly to those of their patients who found the cuisine of the day hard to take. This cuisine was certainly not renowned for its lightness (those recipes which have come down to us are scarcely slimming!). Milk was appreciated for its rustic simplicity, although it was also known that its flavour could be improved by adding aromatic plants to the animals' diet. "Do we prefer milk?", asks Virgil in the *Georgics*, "let us pick laburnum, sweet clover and salty herbs in abundance ourselves and feed them to the animals, [for the sheep] keep a secret salty taste in their milk".

Soft cheese was an everyday food, but there were also salted and matured "long-life" products. As Virgil again explains, "the milk gathered at dawn or during the day is put with rennet overnight. Milk gathered as the shadows are falling and the sun is setting, is carried into town by the shepherd at daybreak in bronze vessels, or it may be sprinkled with a little salt and kept by for the winter." There were two possible sources for the rennet. In addition to the traditional calf's rennet stomach (the fourth compartment of the stomach of ruminants, which secretes the gastric juices), there was also vegetable-based rennet: the sap of the fig or other plants, such as yellow bedstraw, also known as cheese rennet. The curd was sometimes flavoured with thyme or various other aromatic herbs. It was strained slowly using rushwork *faisselles*, then pressed vigorously so that the last of the whey trickled out from it.

A cowherd from Latium. *Museum of Roman Civilisation, Rome.* BELOW: a carved Roman sarcophagus depicting a pastoral scene. *Roman Baths Museum, Rome.*

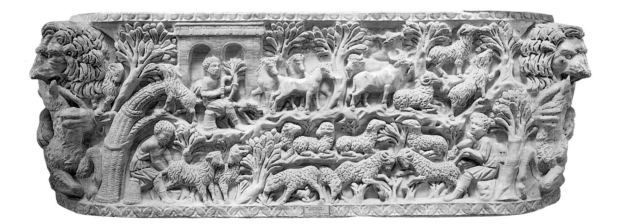

An 11th-century fresco (ABOVE) from the Villa Adriana. *Vatican Museum, Rome.* BELOW: a mythological scene showing the Roman wolf nursing Romulus and Remus, the founders of the eternal city. Detail from a fresco at the *Capitoline Museum, Rome.*

The head of a Roman soldier, 5th-6th century. In his pack (whose top is visible here), every soldier in the legion carried a hunk of cheese. *Mosaics Museum, Topkapi Palace, Istanbul.*

Salting was the best method of preserving cheeses, although they could also be wrapped in the leaves of trees with antiseptic properties. The Romans ate their cheeses at every stage of maturity. When they had become too old and strong, they were left to soak in wine or vinegar with aromatic herbs. This marinated cheese, which was also known to the Greeks, was recommended as an antidote to dysentery and stomach aches, which seem to have been the Romans' great problem. In the 1st century AD Columella gave the following recipe: "Cut up some large chunks of last year's dried sheep's cheese and place them in a pot, covering them completely with the finest quality must, so that the liquid stands higher than the cheese [...]. Seal over the pot as soon as it is filled". The preparation would be ready to taste, or use as seasoning, three weeks later.

In his *Natural History*, from the same period, Pliny wrote glowingly of the pressed and hard cheeses of the Italian peninsula, which already had several centuries of civilisation behind them. Each region had its own products: the Apennines were "fertile in cheeses"; Liguria was specialised in a variety "made with sheep's milk": Etruria was famous for its "Luna" (moon) cheeses, "remarkable for their size, each one weighing up to a thousand pounds" (327 kg). Goat's milk made "a popular cheese whose flavour is greatly enhanced if the fresh cheese is smoked: it is prepared this way in Rome where it is preferred above all others". At the cheese market in Rome, "where the produce of all lands could be compared in one place, the most exalted provincial creations are those of the region around Nîmes, the Lozère and the villages of the Gévaudan". The cheeses of Dalmatia and Savoie were no less acclaimed. But those of Gaul were thought to have "a medicinal taste", unseasoned by either herbs or spices.

Hard cheeses such as Parmesan and Pecorino were made famous by Roman legionnaires, who soon flavoured them with pepper brought from the Far East. The soldiers clearly needed a cheese which kept well and which could stand up to being jolted along in ox-drawn carts over long distances. The Roman road network was the best in the world, but it still took weeks, or even months, to travel across the Empire. The daily ration of the legionnaires was considerably improved when the emperor decided to promote provincial hard cheeses, which were remote ancestors of English Cheshire cheese, Cantal from the Auvergne in France and Beaufort from the Alps.

The rise of commerce and the related development of communication routes gave a natural advantage to those cheeses which travelled well, such as the hard cheeses of the mountain regions of Gaul, the Alps, the Jura and the Massif Central. Over shorter distances, marbled cheeses of the Roquefort type also benefited. But the great barbarian invasions of the 5th century put a temporary brake on this burgeoning cheese industry. As for all the finest fruits of the earth, peacetime was a prerequisite for cheese if it was to develop to its full potential. It takes years to create a good pasture and a lengthy maturing process in ideal conditions demands a stable agricultural world.

THE BARBARIANS

The Nordic races, who were unaware of the existence of either hard cheeses or rennet, were labelled vulgar "milk-drinkers" by the Romans. Like the Scandinavians of today, the Vikings ate a great deal of grilled meat and dried, smoked or salted fish, as well as dairy products. In addition to soured milk, which was easy to prepare and a staple food, the women made butter by churning, and prepared Skyr for the winter. Skyr was a fermented, curdled milk, which was salted and sealed inside large containers.

The Burgundians, who came from the north and settled near Roman villas in the mountains – the Alps, Franche-Comté and Burgundy – and in the upper Rhône valley, also used a great deal of soured milk. They settled down quickly to a sedentary way of life, and were soon converted to agriculture. Through their contact with the indigenous population, who were well-versed in fermenting and maturing techniques, they learned how to make cheese.

A barbarian fighting a Roman soldier. Roman colonisation brought with it the development of vineyards and the spread of cheese-making techniques. *The Louvre, Paris.*

Saint Radegonde
serves food to
her guests (ABOVE).
Monasteries had huge
agricultural domains,
whose produce
was given to pilgrims
and the poor.
10th-11th-century
manuscript.
BELOW: harvest and
sheep-shearing
in the month of July.
16th-century Italian
miniature: *Brevarium
Grimani. Marcinia
Library, Venice.*

THE FRANKS

The Burgundians were not the only ones to inherit expertise of several centuries' standing. The Franks, who had settled in the northern and eastern part of France and in Belgium, had only just discovered rennet and continued to prefer soft and creamy cheeses to the hard cheeses produced in the mountain regions. The lands they colonised therefore remained dedicated to bloomy cheeses like Brie, or washed-rind cheeses, such as Maroilles, Munster and Herve. The emperor Charlemagne, who was a great lover of wine, women and cheese, travelled the length and breadth of his vast empire, keeping a look out for good cheeses. He was partial to the *grands crus* of the day, ensuring that Frisian cheese and Brie de Meaux – cheeses known to his ancestors – reached the table of his palace in Aachen, although it is hard to imagine what state they would have been in. He discovered Roquefort while travelling in the Gévaudan and, from that time on, the local bishop had some sent to him every Christmas. History does not relate the nature of the precautions taken to ensure that the famous blue sheep's cheese arrived in good shape. It may have been packed in a stoneware pot, as cream still is sometimes today.

THE MEDITERRANEAN

In certain regions, cattle never succeeded in ousting sheep and goats. This was the case in Greece, southern Italy, Andalucia, the Mediterranean islands (Sicily, Sardinia, Corsica, Malta, the Balearic Islands and the islands of the Aegean Sea), and in North Africa and the Near East. Neither the Spanish nor the Arabs, who successively conquered the region, had any real influence on the villages perched on the rocky hilltops, accessible only by narrow goat-paths. These insular little communities created their own varieties of goat and sheep's cheese. The production methods used do not seem to have changed, for either soft or hard cheeses, since Homer's day. These cheeses, together with olives, often constituted the only genuinely nutritious element in the diet of those people who did not live within reach of the sea.

A shepherd using the milk from his goats to prepare curds. Byzantine mosaic from the 5th or 6th century. *Mosaics Museum, Topkapi Palace, Istanbul.*

The Ricotta aux Galets ("pebble ricotta") made in Sartène, a Corsican speciality almost unobtainable today, is of the same type as these archaic cheeses, which were being made even before pottery was invented. The milk is heated in a goatskin, or a wooden container, into which scorching-hot pebbles are thrown. When the milk has cooled off, the rennet is added. The Touareg of the Sahara still regularly use this technique, whose origins may lie with the Berbers or the Arabs, but may possibly go right back to prehistoric times. Either way, Ricotta aux Galets bears witness to the age-old practices of Mediterranean shepherds.

THE DAWNING OF THE MIDDLE AGES

The High Middle Ages in the West were marked on the one hand by the proliferation of monastic orders and on the other by the burgeoning of religious sects, such as the Cathars, the Albigenses and the Waldensians, who were soon to be suppressed by the papacy. Every one of these religious movements sought to inculcate the faithful not only with spiritual rules but also with very basic and concrete rules of hygiene, including the regulation of dietary habits. So how much cheese was a Christian allowed to eat?

It was actually banished by the Bogomils and the Cathars, but both sects were soon declared heretical by the papacy. Their rigorous doctrines were based on the teachings of Mani (216-274), the Babylonian apostle of a new church which recognised only two antagonistic principles of Good and Evil. Mani preached the "Good News" in India and the Middle East, following the teaching of a mysterious voice which had ordered man to abstain from wine, meat and any form of sexual relations. The Cathars interpreted his doctrine in a radical way, extending the taboo on animal products to cover milk, and as a result cheese was banned too.

On the other hand, the monastic orders encouraged people to eat cheese, which has always been a food associated with the poor. The rule of Saint Benedict, written in 529, appeared in the form of a little book divided into seventy-three chapters, several of which describe daily life in the monastery in practical detail. The author had lived in the mountains around Rome, where cheese had been the main food of the population for centuries. In Benedictine communities, where the monks divided their time between the study of texts, prayer and manual labour, dairy products and cheeses were considered to be an ideal food, combining simplicity, frugality and energy value. The Benedictines founded congregations all over Europe, establishing themselves in England in the 6th century, the Low Countries and Germany in the following century, and ultimately the Nordic lands too. They adhered strictly to their rule everywhere they went, and so remained faithful to their taste for dairy products. Benedictine abbeys

A shepherd in his tent, by Andrea Pisano, goldsmith, sculptor and architect (early 14th century). *Cathedral Museum, Florence.* OPPOSITE: in medieval imagery, the classical shepherd was replaced by a shepherdess. 15th-century pastoral painting. *National Museum, Trento.*

became rich agricultural centres. The monks kept a herd for their milk, wheatfields for their bread and vineyards for their wine, wherever the climate was suitable. When Charlemagne was crowned emperor in the year 800, these monasteries became centres of civilisation and progress. While the precious manuscripts conserved in them were being painstakingly copied and recopied in one part of the building, the great cheeses of the future were being developed just next door.

Not long after, however, the Middle Ages plunged into a dark period. The Carolingian empire fell apart, and the Norman, Magyar and Saracen invasions had a disastrous effect on the countryside. The fields returned to fallow and the population decreased dramatically. Cheese-making traditions had only two refuges: the monasteries and the mountains. Nonetheless, cheese fared better than wine in surviving the terrors of the millenium.

THE PILGRIMS

The Cistercian order was founded in the 11th century (and reformed in the 12th century by Saint Bernard). Within thirty years, it had established 500 abbeys throughout Europe. Christianity was experiencing an economic revival in the same period, and the great pilgrimage vogue transformed the monks into innkeepers and the abbeys into staging posts. It was no longer enough, as it had been in the Benedictine monasteries, just to keep a herd for the community, which was bound by rules not to eat more than it needed. They were now obliged to feed the travellers too. Cheese was an ideal food for these devout people who walked vast distances in order to pray in front of sacred relics.

Through their observance of strict rules concerning the hygiene and preparation of their wines and cheeses, the monasteries were already unwittingly adopting a policy of *appellation contrôlée* (AOC). Their consistently high-quality products were widely reputed, and soon had their imitators. The communities who made them possessed vast amounts of land. For example, Tamié Abbey, founded in the Alps in 1132, which was at the heart of the renewal of its region, and still makes a form of Reblochon today. A quarter of a century after its foundation, the abbey had a hundred dependencies providing it with grain and cheeses. Each dependency was kept by ten lay brothers, who were monks employed to do agricultural work, such as clearing the forest, raising cattle and sheep and making butter and cheese. The number of cultivated fields continued to grow, and the monks began quite naturally to become interested in using the sunny high mountain slopes for pasture. "The monks devoted themselves to clearing the land, cutting down the trees, tearing out the undergrowth and setting fire to it, fanning the blaze by means of large sticks", relates a chronicler of the period. The maintenance of

the high mountain pastures was gradually taken on by the village communities who bought their autonomy from the abbeys from the 15th century onwards, after the end of the pilgrimages. The alpine meadows were kept up by peasants living in villages situated half-way up the mountains, who observed strict rules to guard against over-grazing. The high mountain pastures were put under collective control, as was the summer cheese-making, and large cheeses were produced. The climatic conditions ensured that the cellars were permanently cool and damp, favouring the production of slow-maturing pressed cheeses, such as Appenzeller, Fontina, Gruyère or Beaufort, which had been popular with the Romans. These could be found in Italy, Switzerland, Austria and France.

MONKS, TRAPPISTS AND REVERENDS

The reputation of the monasteries no longer rested uniquely on the piety of those who lived in them. It was also judged by the products they sold to the outside world to safeguard their own subsistence. These products were essentially their cheeses. Munster, Port-Salut, Maroilles and Saint-Nectaire are all names of abbeys which evoke cheeses with spicy aromas and flavours. 19th-century advertising and publicity would later link these delicate soft cheeses with the image of a ruddy-faced monk, as the symbol of an age-old savoir-faire.

By the end of the Middle Ages, a good many great cheeses were well-established in their native domains. Maroilles Abbey, in the Thiérache region along the border between France and Belgium, had been making and selling a thick square cheese with a washed rind since the year 1000. The peasants too produced the cheese at the request of the abbots, using it as a means to pay their dues. The influence of the establishment extended from the Rhine as far as the English Channel. The other monasteries affiliated to it also made its famous cheese, which became the father of a line of high-tasting cheeses, including the aptly-named Puant Macéré ("Soaked Stinker"), or Gris de Lille, Pont-l'Evêque, Livarot, Munster and, no doubt, Limburger. The monks then took the leftovers of Maroilles cheese – nothing could be wasted – and, blending them with paprika, parsley, tarragon and sometimes whey, they invented the Boulette d'Avesnes, a second-hand product with a first-rate taste.

A round face, bursting with health and high spirits: the typical cheese-label image of the monk as a jolly artisan of country fare.

Italian cheese seller (late 17th century). G M Mitelli. *Biblioteca Nazionale, Florence.*

THE DEVELOPMENT OF TOWNS AND FAIRS

The great cheeses also profited from the upsurge in international exchanges in the 14th century. Fairs, which had first appeared in the 13th century with the spice and cloth trades, linked Venice and Bruges to the major English, German and Scandinavian towns, via the large markets in Champagne. Spices from all over the world were stacked cheek

by jowl beside cheeses of every variety, brought in from the depths of the countryside. Cheese held an important place, even if it did not always travel well. The further a cheese travelled, carried in the luggage of tradesmen, or in pilgrims' bags, the greater its reputation but the harder its rind tended to grow. Others, like Brie, which were omnipresent on all the stalls and inn tables of their own regions, remained provincial jewels, lingering long in the memory of those passing through who tasted them.

The rapidly expanding towns consumed a great deal of agricultural produce. Markets were held in them daily, and the peasants came in to town to offer their wares. Professionals concerned with food quality and taste, whose number included the cheese merchants, set up shop in the cities and organised themselves into guilds. Traders in dairy products could amass an abundant supply from the surrounding regions. Like the local wines and alcohols, all these various cheeses forged their own reputations in the taverns and inns of the town.

An increasing number of spicy cheeses were beginning to appear in northern Europe. This trend would become widespread in the 17th century, when the Dutch East Indies Company began to sell the precious "grains of paradise" (pepper) and the extraordinary clove, among other things, in the ports of the Baltic and the North Sea. Cheeses like Norwegian Nökkelost, Dutch Gouda and Frisian cheese were famous for the extra flavour added by the use of cloves, pepper or cumin.

The Effects of Good Government in the City, by A Lorenzetti. Stock farming, working in the fields and prosperity. *Palazzo Pubblico, Siena.*

Cheese being sold in Alkmaar in the Netherlands (ABOVE). Mid-17th-century painting. *Stedelijk Museum, Amsterdam.* BELOW: the market in Milan, by Alessandro Magnesco (early to mid-18th century).

PROTESTANTS AND CATHOLICS

The Reformation, which broke out in the first half of the 16th century, made Flanders and the northern countries into great lovers of butter. One of the Protestants' demands was for the lifting of the interdicts on food, which made Fridays and the forty days of Lent into fast days. In the space of a century, the taste for cooking with butter swept across England. Fatless cheeses also became popular in the reformed countries, the cream being removed for butter-making. In Catholic countries too, the Church gave its consent to numerous relaxations of the rule. Cooking with pork fat became the norm in the south, and eating butter and full-fat cheeses during Lent was considered ess of an evil.

After the ravages of the One Hundred Years War (1337-1463) which set England against France, and the horrors of the fights between Protestants and Catholics, the countryside was in a sorry condition. The poor peasant had very few cows, even once prosperity began to return. He either left the cows' milk for the calves, which he sold at the market, or used it to make butter, also to be sold. Cheese for his own needs and milk for his children, he took from his goat, which required little in the way of food, and could fend largely for itself on waysides and uncultivated land.

Whether serving to tickle the palate of kings, or to provide much-needed nourishment for the people, cheese and butter were certainly a reflection of the prosperity of a country. Sully, treasurer to Henri IV, summarised the situation at the end of the 16th century, when France was licking the wounds it had sustained in the wars of religion, by a phrase that has remained famous to this day: "ploughing and pasturage are the teats of France".

A French peasant on his way to market to sell his poultry and cheeses. Miniature by Jost Amman (1557). National Library, Madrid.

THE POOR RELATION

Goats were kept above all by poor people, hermits, widows and other have-nots, for whom their milk provided vital nourishment. The old Roman belief in the virtues of goat's milk still held sway. The children of wet-nurses in the service of the aristocracy who were deprived of their mother's milk, were given goat's milk. "For a pittance", wrote Montaigne at the end of the 16th century, "we tear tiny infants out of the arms of their mothers and force the latter to take care of our own [...] And, when they cannot feed their children from their own breasts, [they bring in] goats to the rescue".

There were goats everywhere. It was very rare for a farm not to keep one or two. Their economic value was negligible but their usefulness was undeniable. Goat's cheese was usually restricted to family consumption only, but it occasionally made a name for itself in regions too poor to produce cow's cheese.

THE AGE OF EXPANSION

The French Revolution in 1789 gave birth to one famous cheese: the Camembert. It happened when a priest from Meaux, fleeing from persecution, sought refuge in Normandy with his cousin Marie Harel. She decided to make a cheese according to his description of the method that had been so successful for Brie in his own region. Aided by Napoleon III's enthusiasm for the cheese, the development of the railways and the invention of the round box made of wood shavings, Marie Harel's creation eventually gained worldwide recognition as one of the symbols of France.

People, ideas and tastes were massively stirred up in continental Europe at the beginning of the 19th century as a result of the Napoleonic campaigns. Entire armies travelled across many countries. They were often poorly provisioned and soldiers had to fall back on local produce. Putigny, a soldier of the old guard of Napoleon I, who was later made a baron of the empire for his feats of arms, was once so racked by hunger that he escaped from the hospital where he was being cared for and came back with bread, cheese and wine. Looking back, he recounted the welcome he had received from the inhabitants of Flushing in the Netherlands: "The soup was pantagruelian: two pounds of white bread per day, a pound of meat, some creamy cheese, and good beer and brandy".

By the mid-19th century, industrialisation was encouraging the peasants to flood into the urban centres. In the cities, they tended to collect in pockets of people from the same region, nostalgically trying to remain faithful to their customs, and above all to the culinary traditions and products of their own region. The development of the railways had a truly revolutionary impact on the history of cheese. By enabling even the most fragile cheeses to travel long distances and still look and taste their best in faraway markets, the train contributed to the dissemination of cheeses throughout Europe. Things had come a long way since the days when cheese used to be transported in straw-filled barrels, a process requiring

A vendor of milk products and cream cheeses, 1900. *Bibliothèque Nationale, Paris.* OPPOSITE ABOVE: poster from 1902. *Bibliothèque Nationale, Paris.* OPPOSITE BELOW: poster from 1914. *Bibliothèque Nationale, Paris.*

The railway made it possible for regional products to be transported long distances, improving the quality of goods available in the cities. Epinal engraving (1845-1850). *Epinal Collection, Bibliothèque Nationale, Paris.*

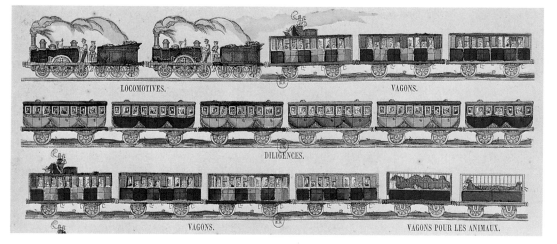

LOCOMOTIVES.   VAGONS.

DILIGENCES.

VAGONS.   VAGONS POUR LES ANIMAUX.

infinite precautions. Amateurs of cheese, already familiar with hard (Parmesan) and semi-hard cheeses (Edam, Gouda, Emmental, Beaufort, Cantal, Tilsit), could now savour soft bloomy cheeses (Camembert, Brie, Chaource) washed-rind cheeses (Limburger, Munster, Epoisses) and try marbled cheeses (Roquefort and various blue cheeses) unspoiled by the jolting and the long journey times of travel by road. Cheeses became an essential part of the economy, each one acquiring its own name and devotees.

THE CONQUEST OF THE NEW WORLDS

Through the 17th, 18th and 19th centuries, the New Worlds of North and South America, Australia and New Zealand attracted large numbers of immigrants. It was not only families in search of a promised land, ex-convicts on the run and poor onlookers swept up by silver-tongued recruiting sergeants, that set sail in the ships bound for these places. Their holds too were filled with poultry, pigs, sheep, goats and cattle intended as provisions for the colonies being set up on what was believed to be virgin land. Milk for cheese-making was therefore available to the settlers from the first, but for a long time, they made only a simple, household soft cheese. In North America and Australia, cheese-making went straight from this domestic level to industrial production, while old Europe, with its traditional markets and its hundred-year-old pastures, kept its prerogative on rurally-produced cheeses. The mechanised process of cheddarisation spread rapidly in all English-speaking countries. Besides being a feast for the senses, cheese also became a functional and abundant food. So abundant was it that Canada attracted

Wooden cheese boxes were seized on as a support for imagery intended to glorify the cheese: monks, famous people, Norman villages, etc.

A cheese competition, as seen by Cham, a caricaturist. BELOW: emigrants to the New World took cows with them to ensure a supply of milk and cheese while they awaited the first harvest. The Rocky Mountains, F Palmer (19th century). American Museum, Bath.

CHEESE AND CIVILISATION

The giant Cheddar "The Canadian Mite" pulled by six horses at the end of the 19th century: the era of national, international and "universal" exhibitions.

OPPOSITE: individual cheeses being sold at the Baltard food halls, Paris, 1950.

attention at the end of the last century by successfully producing a Cheddar weighing 10 tonnes.

The influx of expatriates from the great cheese-producing countries of Europe, in particular from Italy, led to an increase in diversity in cheeses in the New World. Cheese was clearly indispensable to the cuisines of these immigrants. Who can imagine a soufflé or a gratin without Gruyère, pasta without Parmesan, a pizza without Mozzarella, or a Greek salad without Feta? Italian restaurants multiplied in the big cities of North America, Australia, Argentina and Chile between the wars, and the taste for cheeses from the peninsula became widespread. More recently, cheeses made from unpasteurised milk following ancient methods but using modern materials have been brought back into favour by the hippy movement. As a result, new varieties of cheese appeared in California and Australia in the 1960s and 1970s.

In Europe mechanisation, dairy-based production and pasteurisation have led to more stable cheeses, which are easier to commercialise and export, but their original flavours have been banalised in the process. The natural ferments which gave Camemberts and Epoisses the full subtlety of their flavour, whether mild or spicy, are no longer used. The international cheese trade brings with it new regulations. It has led to the adoption of strict laws governing hygiene and the spreading of the micro-organisms which cheeses made with unpasteurised milk carry by definition. These harmless micro-organisms, which vigilant master cheese-makers have had well under control for centuries, are in fact the source of the products' particular qualities of flavour. Eliminating them by pasteurisation destroys the very element responsible for the distinctive taste of "real cheeses". Will a day come when gourmets take to the streets in angry protest, demanding protection rights for cheeses and carrying banners calling for the rights of Munster and Remoudou to smell, and the rights of Roquefort, Stilton and Gorgonzola to be mouldy?

44

CHEESE PRODUCTION

C heese cannot really be said to have been "invented". This exquisite food must have resulted from the simple observation that milk left in a container ends up by coagulating, even more so if it is hot. All that is required to obtain a compact and delicious substance is to drain the curds in a mould (from the Latin *formaticum*, giving the Italian *formaggio*, and the French *forme* and *fromage*). One of the first everyday objects made by man and used to filter the curds was the wicker draining-basket. As to the recipient for the milk, our ancestors used what nature offered them: either the calabash or bits of gouged-out wood made perfect moulds. Milk, pasture, cow, sheep and goat are to cheese what grape, soil and variety are to wine. Unless this is fully grasped, it is impossible to understand the difference between an industrial and a farmhouse cheese, or a bottle of plonk and a *grand cru classé*. Over thousands of years, like alchemists of a bygone age, the cheese-maker has pushed his craft to its limits and produced a multi-coloured cheese-board of different savours.

INTERNATIONAL REGULATIONS

In the 1930s, cheese-making countries tried hard to establish regulations, for reasons both of hygiene and of trade. They began by giving cheese a definition recognised in law, such as in Belgium in 1932 or France in 1935. After the Second World War, and along with the development of international trade in dairy products, it became necessary to harmonise the various national legislations. In 1952, the major cheese-making countries signed the first "Stresa Convention" which stipulates that the word "cheese is reserved for products, whether fermented or not, obtained by drainage after coagulation of the milk, cream, semi-skimmed or skimmed milk, or mixture of these, as well as any product obtained by partial concentration of lactoserum or buttermilk, and excluding, in all cases, any addition of fat foreign to the milk". The code of principles of the FAO and the WHO provided a similar definition in 1963, specifying further that it be a fresh or matured product; this standard has been accepted by all countries concerned. The aim of the Stresa Convention was also to guarantee the appellation of certain cheeses abroad and hence prevent imitations. It thus forbids countries not the original producers of the products protected by the Convention to export a cheese whose appellation is protected without clearly stating the country in which it is manufactured. For example, "Made in Denmark" Camembert can be found. Four cheeses, however, are given absolute protection. This means that only the original producer countries have the right to manufacture them. They are France's Roquefort, Italy's Pecorino Romano and Fiore Sardo, and Switzerland's Sbrinz.

The label of this "Brie", made in the United States, boasts a French name and an image of a French château to complete the illusion. PRECEDING PAGES: cheese-making is a job for the whole family in this engraving by the Dutch artist, Gustav van Woltters.

"Absolutely Pure Milk".

The advantage of the *appellations contrôlées*, or AOCs, which provide the connoisseur with a guarantee and the producer with a prestigious brand name, is that they preserve cheese-making traditions and the respect of certain craft techniques. Still, preparation for the Single European Market has somewhat upset this legal construction and triggered off debate between the agriculturally modern countries producing cheeses industrially from pasteurised milk and those in the south of Europe – with Italy, France and Spain in the fore – fighting to save their raw-milk farmhouse cheeses and, hence, their small farmers' livelihoods.

The quality of a cheese inevitably depends on that of the raw material: milk. AOC and, generally, farmhouse cheeses are manufactured on the same premises as the milking, using milk from the last one or two milking sessions which has undergone no processing whatsoever. With the implementation of European regulations, certain countries systematically recommend the use of pasteurised milk, better suited to standards of hygiene. Pasteurisation consists in heating milk very rapidly to a temperature of 90° C, then cooling it immediately, in order to destroy pathogenic germs. As the cheese-making industry developed, this became necessary because milk was not only being collected from various sources and could not be processed quickly enough, but also had to undergo a number of manipulations. The pasteurised milk is then seeded with only those strains of micro-organism required for cheese-making. Since pasteurisation denatures some of the solid proteins and risks making coagulation impossible, nowadays, heating to about 70° C, a sort of mild pasteurisation, is preferred. This renders the germs inactive for a certain time, during which the milk must be seeded quickly.

Sterilising the milk churns to kill any germs which may cause the milk to go bad. Detail from an early 20th-century engraving.

Nevertheless, it should still be mentioned that the problems arising over the past few years were actually caused by cheeses made from milk, either pasteurised or from indeterminate sources, which had not been processed within the required time-frame. Pasteurisation does not in fact totally eliminate all possibility of contamination since, by destroying the milk's natural flora, it allows any harmful germ to proliferate very rapidly as there is no longer any "competition". Another consequence is that it destroys a certain number of vitamins contained in the milk and also blurs the originality of each milk type and hence the cheese's individual taste. As for the traditional methods – tried and tested for centuries – although they may not be applied industrially, they do nevertheless remain perfectly acceptable for farmhouse cheeses. With supporters of farmhouse cheeses in one camp, and partisans of industrial products in the other, the big question today is how the Common Market will affect the situation.

British Stilton (ABOVE) and Swiss Emmental (BOTTOM CENTRE) authenticity stamps. BOTTOM LEFT: all *grana* cheeses, which include Parmigiano Reggiano, are protected by a clearly-defined AOC, set up by the Stresa Convention (1952), and a series of Italian laws. BOTTOM RIGHT: the identification code and "Holland" stamp are clearly visible on this Boererkaas, the name generally given to Gouda made with unpasteurised milk.

LEGISLATION IN DIFFERENT COUNTRIES

Over and above international legislation, each country has its own laws concerning its own products. In Great Britain, where cheese-making legislation is little developed, farmhouse-producers of Cheshire, Cheddar and Lancashire have got together and rendered the "English Farmhouse Cheese" label compulsory, in order to protect their regional cheeses' specificity. Even so, each manufacturer still keeps his recipes a closely-guarded secret to ensure his cheese remains different from his neighbour's. The only English cheese protected up to now is Stilton: the milk comes from the local area and manufacturing methods are traditional, but there are no rules as to the use of raw milk or not. In Italy, gastronomic craftsmanship has long had its custodians. Cheeses are protected by AOC supervisory associations. The main associations have had cheeses such as Asiago, Fontina, Gorgonzola, Grana Padano, and Parmigiano Reggiano listed after the manner of historic buildings. Switzerland, too, applies its "Switzerland" stamp of guarantee on its major cheeses: Emmental, Sbrinz, Tête de Moine, Gruyère, Royalp-Tilsit, Appenzeller and Fribourg. In Spain, by listing seven of its cheeses, Roncal, Mahon, Manchego, Liebana Picon, Cabrales, Cantabria and Idiazabal, the survival of Manchega and Manech sheep has been ensured. Portugal is trying to save its delicious cheeses by listing the most remarkable among them: Azeitão, Serra, Serpa and Ilha. By doing this, they are also giving the small dairy producers the chance to survive the threat posed by industrial dairies. Holland protects its Gouda, Edam and Maasdam by its "Holland" stamp and a code of identification in the form of a film made using casein integrated into the rind. Scandinavian countries, and especially Denmark – a big exporter – have regulated the manufacture of their cheeses by strict legislation on hygiene. And this is the rule for all other countries recently embarked upon cheese-making: the United States, Canada, Australia and New Zealand. The eastern countries have not yet made the necessary legislation, neither has South America nor most of the rest of the world.

As the above show, true Camembert used to be the object of the most fanciful forgeries. It was not until 1983 that Normandy Camembert was granted an AOC.

The AOCs are far from representing the immense wealth of cheeses in a given country. It is nigh on impossible to carry out a census of all existing cheeses, and out of the question for those that have disappeared. If all the speciality cheeses are included, the figure becomes enormous. Consequently, there are many hidden treasures in every European country that cheese-lovers will never hear about as a result of industrialisation and marketability.

FRENCH LEGISLATION

In France, legislation did not start with today's authorities. When a cheese had the good fortune to please a king or an emperor and find its way onto his table, or when it was part of the tithe payable to a lord or monastery, its individuality had to be maintained for its privileges to continue. Nobody thought of deceiving Charlemagne with a different-quality Comté or, 600 years later, Charles VI as to what Roquefort should taste like. It was Charles VI who first gave the inhabitants of Roquefort the monopoly for this famous cheese, two of which have been offered every year to the monks of the nearby Abbey of Conques since 1070. Later on, the Parliament of Toulouse protected this great cheese against imitations and made it illegal to "call them Roquefort under penalty of a fine of one thousand pounds and prosecution". Moving on from special charters and trading-licences, the first written legislation concerning the protection of cheese occurred in 1925 for Roquefort: only cheeses matured in the Roquefort caves were entitled to this prestigious name. The legislation was consolidated by a decree in 1966, and is still in force, entailing a fine or prison sentence to whosoever attempts to counterfeit this AOC. Nowadays, there are a large number of laws defining the various AOCs. They are far stricter than the international conventions regarding the source of the milk, and define in very precise terms the regions authorised to supply milk for such and such a cheese. The total number of AOC cheeses in France in 1992 was thirty-two, and every year more traditional cheeses apply for AOC status. The legislators have complemented international conventions by various texts; the decree of 1988, taking the future Single Market into consideration, represents the current basis for the regulation of French cheese-making. The type of milk used must be stated on the label and the absence of this indicates that the milk is cow's. The source of milk for all goat's or sheep's cheeses must be given. Cheese called "de chèvre" must contain no other milk type. Similarly, a "mi-chèvre" goat's cheese must contain at least one quarter's worth of goat's milk. The percentage of fat determines the qualifier: "triple-cream" for 75% and over; "double-cream" for 60 to 75%; "cream", 50 to 60%; "low-fat" (allégé), 20 to 30%; "fatless" (maigre), less than 20%; and "made from skimmed milk", 0%. Similarly, the minimum level of dry matter must be 23 g per 100 g of cheese.

The Maroilles Seller: unpackaged, unlabelled cheeses. Colour lithograph by Delpech, late 19th century. Cabinet des Estampes, Musée Carnavalet, Paris.

A s we saw earlier, the hundreds of different types of cheese can be differentiated both by the type of milk – raw, skimmed or pasteurised; and by the animal – cow, goat, sheep, buffalo or even horse and camel. Similarly, the various characteristics of cheese-making also separate cheese into a number of families. For all of them however, there are four major stages in the basic process: (1) curdling or coagulation of the milk (2) shaping of the curds (de-moulding and draining) (3) salting, washing and seeding (4) maturing.

CURDLING OR COAGULATION OF THE MILK

Casein, a protein present in large quantities in mammalian milk, coagulates naturally in an acid medium: left to stand in a recipient, the milk can spontaneously turn from a liquid to a solid through the action of the natural ferments (lactic ferments) it contains and which develop on the sugar found in the milk, the lactose. This sour milk is the first type of soft cheese man must have tried. Natural coagulation is difficult to regulate, but it can be triggered off by adding rennet. Fast and homogeneous coagulation, producing firm curds, may be obtained with various substances: the rennet, for example, of calves or kids. This little stomach pouch found in all ruminants secretes the gastric juices. In the Roman epoch, the rennet of wild animals such as deer was preferred. Whereas before, it used to be used in strips, nowadays, when chemical rennet is not used instead, it is produced as a liquid or powder. In very poor regions around the Mediterranean basin or on islands where sheep and goats are too precious as livestock to kill for the rennet, vegetable rennets, thistles or fig-tree sap, are used. Most farmhouse sheep's cheeses made on the Iberian peninsula or Mediterranean islands are still

The Cheesemonger. Painting by André Fougeron, 1952. *Private collection* (OPPOSITE). Right: Parmesan-making. The milk is heated in copper cauldrons which can contain up to 725 kg. Firm-textured curds are then produced by adding a culture of heat-resistant lactobacillae and *Streptococcus thermophilus*, plus water-diluted rennet, to the milk.

M aking Stilton. Removing a heat coil from a pan of raw milk, after it has heated the milk by steaming. The milk is now ready for renneting.

Making cheese: the varicus stages. (This sequence of illustrations reads from left to right, and from top to bottom, across the double spread.) TOP ROW (1) heating the milk in copper cauldrons at a dairy in Savoie. (2) cutting up the curds for Parmesan. (3) preparing to lift the curd out of the vat in a canvas cloth. (4) a canvas-wrapped mass of curd is lifted out of the vat using a pulley.

Separating the curds during the making of Pont-L'Evêque cheese (MIDDLE ROW, 1). (2) putting the broken-up curds into the moulds. (3) Comté goes under the press. (4) the second pressing. BOTTOM ROW (1) brushing the rind of Bethmale cheese. (2) Maroilles being salted in a vat of brine. (3) a specialist testing Cheddar in the maturing cellars. (4) overseeing the maturation of Camemberts.

made with this type of rennet. Elsewhere, in Great Britain, Australia, the United States or Holland, cheeses based on vegetable rennet are made, to cater for a vegetarian clientele.

Renneting consists in adding the rennet to the heated milk. The amount used and the temperature depend on each other and also on the acidity of the milk (generally, skimmed milk from the day before to which the next morning's milk is added, or the fattier milk of a single milking). This operation requires enormous know-how. Coagulation, which cannot take place under 10° C, is activated at temperatures between 20 and 40° C. According to the type of cheese, the milk is brought to a temperature of between 25 and 36° C. The time taken for the milk to coagulate varies from under 30 minutes (25 for Tomme de Savoie) to 36 hours (for Cabécou which is renneted at an ambient temperature). At this stage, the milk is broken down into a solid (the curds) and a liquid (whey, or lactoserum).

SHAPING OF THE CURDS

Once the curds have formed, the whey must be removed to obtain a firmer substance. To start with, the curds are broken down in a vat to separate the curds from the whey, or lactoserum, by means of a "curd-cutter". The curds are cut up into lumps of different sizes according to the type of cheese: the harder the cheese, the smaller the lumps must be. The curd mass is constantly stirred to prevent it from agglomerating again. This technique, mechanised in the last century for the manufacture of Cheddar, for example, allows the draining operations to be shortened. The duration of this cutting-up, or "de-curding", period also varies according to the cheese, but must not exceed certain limits above which the substance becomes acid. It is during this operation that the curds of hard cheeses such as Parmesan or Comté are heated in large copper vats where they coagulate to obtain a more compact consistency. They are heated to less than 55° C (39° C for pressed, semi-hard cheeses) since, at over this temperature, the lactic ferments no longer function and the result is a sort of pasteurised curds.

There are several methods for removing the curds from the vat for draining. For cheeses like Maroilles, Herve, Remoudou or goat's cheeses, a large, sloping draining-board covered in long

Enamelled mould for shaping cheese, from the end of the 16th century (ABOVE). *Musée des Arts Décoratifs, Paris.* OPPOSITE: students learning the various stages of cheese-making at the University of Wisconsin School of Agriculture in the 1920s (TOP). BOTTOM: making "Swiss cheese" (dipping the curds) at Jorden Cheese factory, Brodhead, Wisconsin, 1914.

Transferring the curds from the vat directly to the moulds (RIGHT). FAR RIGHT: fresh Munsters and, behind them, their moulds.

Farmhouse cheese production. Preparing the curds for Laguiole cheese, made in the Aubrac region of France (TOP LEFT).

TOP RIGHT: draining and breaking up the curds.

BOTTOM LEFT: small Cabécous or goats' cheeses being moulded by hand.

BOTTOM RIGHT: Saint-Nectaire cheeses being pressed into shape in their moulds, on a table with a gutter to let the whey run off.

grooves is used and the entire vat poured onto it. Ladles may also be used to transfer the curds directly into moulds containing holes through which the whey can run off. This is the technique used for Roquefort or Fourme d'Ambert. For pressed, semi-hard cheeses like Beaufort or Emmental, the traditional method has been to use a large, strong cloth which allows the whey to filter through the holes and retains the curds. Other cheeses, like Camembert for example, are made from unbroken curds which are moulded directly: very carefully, the curds are scooped up in a ladle and put into a recipient with holes. To make a traditional Camembert, five ladlefuls are needed.

For the pressed cheeses, the draining is speeded up by placing the curds-laden cloth straight into a mould (a bottomless hoop) and pressing it as is. Pressing techniques vary from simply putting a stone on top of the board covering the cheese to piling the cheeses one on top of the other. For many years, the most common method was to use a lever press with sliding weights positioned along the arm to increase the pressure. More and more often today, even though traditional cheeses are still pressed according to old-fashioned methods, the big dairies are tending to use hydraulic presses. As the whey runs off, the pressure is increased. While this is happening, the cheeses are turned over several times to ensure they drain to the same extent on both sides. This is also done with non-pressed cheeses: the cheese is turned over in the mould while it is still moist enough and removed when it reaches the right degree of hardness. For some cheeses, such as those from the Balearic Islands, the cloth is tightened as the curds solidify and acts as the mould, giving the cheese its final shape.

SALTING, WASHING AND SEEDING

Salting may be done in the vat, as it is for Cantal, or, more usually, when taken out of the mould. Salting serves a number of functions: it speeds up the drying process, heightens the cheese's flavour, helps the rind to form and slows down the proliferation of micro-organisms, thus enhancing the cheese's

Cheese moulds being made in Bethmale, near Foix (BELOW). TOP LEFT: Tomme de Savoie cheeses being put into

moulds in a mountain chalet. *L'Illustration, 1853.* TOP RIGHT: putting Edam into moulds. Drawing by F de Maenen, *circa* 1910.

durability. The salting technique most commonly used, and preferred by most cheese-makers because of its practicality, is immersion in a brine bath. It also has the advantages of not requiring the cheese be turned over constantly, as in dry-salting, and of ensuring its complete impregnation. On average, this takes from two to four days, but only half an hour for Livarot and up to five days for Bleu de Gex. Depending on the cheese, the brine will contain between 250 and 350 g salt per litre. Some rindless cheeses, like Feta, are always kept in a low-salt brine. Dry-salting consists in rubbing the cheese with salt on repeated occasions after it has been removed from the mould. The use of cooking-salt gives the thick rinds found on Emmental and Beaufort, and, thanks to their hardness and rigidity, these large cheeses, weighing over 50 kg, can be lifted and moved without splitting. Washed-rind cheeses, like Maroilles, are brushed or washed with salt at regular intervals during their maturation, preventing the formation of mould and keeping the rind soft. Some cheeses end their maturation by being washed (or bathed) in spirits. This is done to Epoisses, which is washed in white wine and marc de Bourgogne, or Remoudou, which is sometimes washed in beer.

Some cheeses are seeded with fungus to produce the soft white down of their "bloomy" rind, or the blue/green veining of "blue" cheeses. Camembert is pulverised with *Penicillium candidum* then placed in a drying-room for four days during which its typical "fur" develops. Roquefort is pierced with a long needle some thirty times; this not only introduces the *Penicillium roqueforti* spores, but also aerates the cheeses, allowing the mould to grow. Various flavouring agents may also be added to the curds, as they are for Gouda, or, if they are on the outside, as they are for Boulette d'Avesnes, they are added just before the maturing starts.

MATURING

For soft or semi-hard cheeses, the stay in the drying-room is a preliminary to maturation. Generally lasting two days, it allows any excess humidity on the rind to be eliminated. Increasingly often though, cheese-makers are systematically putting their cheeses in drying-rooms to speed up the

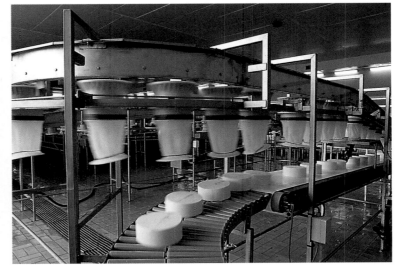

maturation. Maturation itself is carried out in cellars where the hygrometry and temperature are constant, with these factors playing a determining role in the amount of flavour the cheese will have, and in its consistency. Cellars are the best place for maturing cheeses because the temperature and humidity are stable. Temperate cellars (12 to 15° C) speed up the maturation and are especially used for washed-rind cheeses like Reblochon. The hygrometry is close to 90%. Slow-maturing cheeses (five months or more) like Beaufort are matured in cool cellars (8 to 10° C) with a similar hygrometry of about 90%. Other than cellars, humid, ventilated rooms, often called drying-rooms, are used for goat's cheeses especially. Only cheeses intended for consumption when very dry, like Sbrinz and Parmesan, are matured at ambient temperatures.

No matter how tasty they are, cheeses will soon lose their qualities if not packaged suitably; like wine, they do not travel well. Various types of packaging are used according to whether the milk was raw or pasteurised, and whether the maturation has been completed or not. Bloomy-rind cheeses like Camembert, which continue to mature out of the cellar, are wrapped up in waxed paper and put into wooden boxes: this means the cheese can still breathe. Washed-rind cheeses which stop maturing when they leave the cellar are often wrapped in plastic and retain their humidity and *bouquet*. Soft, natural-rind cheeses (or certain bloomy-rind cheeses such as Brie) may be sold unpackaged, wrapped in a leaf from a tree (Banon) or coated in ash (goat's). Often, they travel on a bed of straw which allows the bottom to continue breathing. European health regulations require that cheese-makers use artificial straw nowadays (which most connoisseurs deplore), or that a sheet of waxed paper be intercalated between the straw and the cheese. Like many soft cheeses, a good number of blue cheeses are sold wrapped up, most often in a sheet of aluminium foil, to prevent the rind from drying out. Semi-hard or hard cheeses are sometimes coated in a waxy film which keeps them smooth (e.g. Dutch cheeses). Mountain cheeses (Comté, Gruyère and Beaufort) are often sold as they are, sometimes with a label stuck on the rind, or with the control stamp either moulded or printed onto the rind itself.

Brie in its wooden box, which serves not only as packaging, but also allows the cheese to breathe and continue to mature, even after it has left the cellar and is displayed in the shop.

Measuring the progress of the "blueing" during the maturation of Roquefort cheese (BOTTOM LEFT). BOTTOM CENTRE: maturation cellars for Neufchâtel cheeses. BOTTOM RIGHT: in the maturation cellars in the Doubs region of France. OPPOSITE: this piece of cheese is 14 years old, as is the overpowering smell released when the top of the airtight bottle is removed.

Sheep's cheese is more of a Mediterranean affair. Most cheeses from the Iberian peninsula, the Mediterranean islands (Corsica, Sardinia, Sicily and the Greek isles) and Italy (excluding the Alps) are sheep's milk cheeses. Their manufacture dates far back into antiquity; requiring little milk, they were easy to make. Sheep's cheeses are sometimes eaten hard as rock, a heritage from the days when they had to be kept to last out the winter. Since their smell became rather overpowering at this stage, they are stored in recipients filled with aromatic olive oil. To make these natural-rind cheeses, the milk is heated to 30° C, then the curds are cut up and moulded. Goat's cheeses come in very characteristic shapes: pyramids, logs, "droppings", "trouser buttons", etc.

PROCESSED CHEESES

These are the result of melting one or more pressed, cooked or uncooked cheeses, and adding milk, cream, butter and sometimes flavouring agents. Metton, Gjetost and Schabzieger are but some of these so-called "re-cooked" cheeses. To obtain *metton*, the basic ingredient of Cancoillotte, the famous speciality from the Franche-Comté, the whey from Comté is boiled until a flaky matter forms at the surface. This is skimmed off, drained and left to ferment until the cheese is impregnated with green mould. It is then used to make the Cancoillotte by melting it with salt-water and butter. Switzerland's Schabzieger is also derived from the manufacture of big pressed mountain cheeses. It owes its nickname of "green cheese" to the meadow fenugreek mixed into it. This zero-fat cheese with its truncated-cone shape is dried, then reduced to powder. Norway's Gjetost contains only a small amount of fat. Made from goat's milk (*Gjet* is goat in Norwegian), but very often mixed with cow's, it is also nicknamed "brown cheese" because of the colour the skimmed milk takes on during cooking. The moulds in which it is made are often imprinted with motifs giving the surface a relief and making it look like an artistically-decorated cake which can be kept for a very long time. It is eaten in the winter and, in the past, Norwegian sailors used to take it with them on their long voyages.

Kernhem, a recently-created Dutch processed cheese (ABOVE). BOTTOM LEFT: goat's milk Fromage Blanc (soft white cheese) from the Berry region of France. BOTTOM CENTRE: Fromage Blanc in a *faisselle* or cheese-drainer. BOTTOM RIGHT: fresh goat's milk cheese.

Then and now; the changing face of cheese-making in the 20th century (OPPOSITE). TOP: details of the interior of a dairy in about 1900, from a watercolour by A Dressel. BOTTOM: the mechanised state of cheese production in 1993. Munsters just out of the press, and after washing.

NORTHERN EUROPE

with a view to producing milk of high quality and local character from old breeds of cattle, and from goats and ewes. They used the milk raw for new cheeses of their own devising and for revivals. In 1985 the European Economic Community woke up to the fact that it had been paying unconscionably to keep up milk prices and buy and stock unsalable butter, block-cheese and milk-powder. Instead of cutting excessive fertiliser use and ending production of lower-quality milk, butter and cheese, the EEC's rigid Milk Quota cut production right across the board. The rare-breed organic farmer, cherishing the countryside and struggling to keep up with a growing demand, had to reduce his herd instead of increasing it. The special local character of his milk makes his product unique, so he cannot buy suitable milk elsewhere. Chemical fertilisers and sprays, as the world's greatest expert, the late Dr. George Cooke told me, "have ironed out the differences between pastures". They nullify the aromatic esters in the herbage, robbing local milk and cheese of most of their character. It also seems likely that by killing much of the healthy natural bacterial population in the soil, they encourage listeria. It is significant that consistently listeria-free milk samples have come from organic farms in one great cheese-making region. Futhermore, animal health is better on organic farms, for which the American Department of Agriculture has evidence, confirmed by experience on British organic farms.

The factory producer can turn anywhere for more milk. He can buy up a flourishing artisan cheese dairy, close it, kill off the rival cheese and divert the milk supplies to increase production of his own characterless extruded-curd. (France has lost several famous cheeses in this way.)

With the whole future of farming at stake, it is madness to hobble cheese-makers who produce what the discriminating public demands and will pay for. Their organic methods maintain, on clean soil, multi-species permanent pastures for grazing, meadows for winter hay, and hedgerows and trees for animal shelter. The approaches to a good cheese farm are rich in flowers (fifty or more species to a field, not counting grasses), bees and varieties of butterflies, and in the bird-song of nature's own pest-controllers. Such farming must be encouraged again in northern Europe, helped, not hindered by the EEC.

This is not foolish sentiment; it is based on scientific fact. The aromas which attract the bees and butterflies (so important to horticulture through pollination) are channelled by the plant oils into the grazing animals' fat and milk. This is the secret of aroma and flavour in cheese. In our Europe of polluted foliage, earth and water and eroded soil, organic farming makes aesthetic, gastronomic and economic sense. Public insistence on real cheese can enrich our diet and turn our pasturelands back into real countryside once more.

Farmhouse Cheddar.
OPPOSITE: a herd of dairy cattle in Surrey, a dairy-farming county.

Dairy produce and cheese market in Chippenham in 1850.

CHEDDAR

This is one of Britain's most popular cheeses. It is named after the village of Cheddar and Cheddar Gorge in Somerset, south-west England. Writing in 1655, Thomas Fuller described it as "the biggest and best of English cheeses". In olden times, this imposing 28-kg cylinder was made on the farm and its fat content depended very much on the farmer's wealth. If he was poor, he used all his cream to make butter for sale in town. The whole-milk Cheddar sold in the markets only found its way to the rich man's table. It differed from the poor man's Cheddar in its creamy-yellow colour. To imitate this colour, people started colouring skimmed-milk Cheddar with a touch of saffron. In the 17th century, this was replaced by anatto, a colouring-agent from a West Indian tree. It also cost less. The same method was later used

Cheddar in storage (BELOW). TOP: cheese cellar. Small "Truckles". Wells Stores, Streatley. FAR RIGHT: Cheddar.

for other cheeses such as Leicester and Cheshire. Although the Cheddar intended for export or manufactured abroad is often of a reddish colour, there are never any colouring-agents in real Cheddar.

In the mid-19th century, Joseph Harding transformed the Cheddar industry from a hand-made to a machine-made process. Industrialisation had arrived, and this very old local cheese was put on the bandwagon. New methods enabled larger amounts of milk to be processed in one go, and hence increased production. Maturation was reduced to a couple of months although the quality remained the same. This shorter maturation period was acheived by the use of higher temperatures, which speed up the process. There were (and still are) however, some producers who continued to keep their cheeses from nine months to two years.

It was only in the 1960s that the major industrial producers began to use pasteurisation and abandoned traditional production methods, thereby depriving Cheddar cheese, along with all the other industrially-made British cheeses, of its true flavour.

Still made in Somerset, Devon and Dorset, Cheddar is now copied almost everywhere: Austria, Belgium, Canada, Denmark, Holland, New Zealand and elsewhere, even Africa.

■ CHEDDAR

Cow's milk cheese (48% fat)

TYPE: pressed, uncooked, semi-hard; dry rind

SHAPE: round, 40 cm in diameter, 40 cm high. Also available in slabs

WEIGHT: from 2 to 25 kg and more

MATURATION: 3 to 6 months on average, but up to 2 years

PRESENTATION: wrapped in cloth

CHESHIRE

Weighing in at a respectable 22 kg, Cheshire, or Chester as they call it in France and Belgium, is made in the area around Chester and neighbouring counties, Shropshire in particular. This very old cheese is said to date back to Celtic times and gourmets throughout the ages have never stopped singing its praises. Its outstanding quality is due to the origin of the milk used: the slightly salty pasture-land around the county-town of Cheshire on the Welsh border. Almost all traditional white and coloured Cheshire today is cloth-bound and waxed. The best farms use raw milk, and Abbey Farm Hawkstone, in Shropshire, maintains the longstanding tradition of using unwaxed cloth. Such cheeses can be rich but not sharp at 18 months, and may develop Green Fade, the old Cheshire term for blueing (explained by the mixing of greeeny-blue mould with apricot coloured cheese). Cheshires are harder and more uniform

today, so Green Fade has become rare. It has given way to a notable new cheese, the purpose-built, raw-milk, coloured BLUE CHESHIRE of Hinton Bank Farm, Whitchurch, in Shropshire. Lightly-pressed, calico-skinned, and pierced by air-jets, not needles, it matures in 21/2 months to a greater strength than the older Green Fade. A softer Cheshire was made on some farms a century ago, for which curds were set aside daily to add to the next day's fresh curds; this was in fact the Stilton method of blueing and indeed it was called "Stilton Cheshire". Under this name Patrick Rance sold its modern, coloured successor, SHROPSHIRE BLUE. Invented by a Stilton-maker in Scotland, and never actually made in Shropshire, it is now produced at Long Clawson Stilton Dairy in Leicestershire.

■ CHESHIRE

Cow's milk cheese (48% fat)

TYPE: pressed, uncooked, semi-hard,

natural rind, wrapped in canvas, waxed or unwaxed

SHAPE: round, the largest are 35 cm in diameter, 40 cm high

WEIGHT: 1, 2, 5, 20 or 22 kg

MATURATION: 3 to 6 months, or more for non-waxed versions

DERBY

This mild and delicate cheese used to be a speciality of Derbyshire in the British Midlands. Nowadays it is made using pasteurised milk. Maturing generally takes some 2 to 3 months but can also be prolonged for up to a year to obtain a slightly pungent taste, a little like Lancashire cheese, although its texture is less crumbly.

■ DERBY

Pasteurised cow's milk cheese (48% fat)

TYPE: pressed, uncooked, semi-hard, natural rind

SHAPE: round, 38 cm in diameter, 12 cm high

Blue Cheshire (ABOVE AND LEFT). Needles have been inserted to allow the mould into the cheese so that it blues. TOP LEFT: farmhouse production of Cheddar cheese. BOTTOM: Cheshire.

WEIGHT: 14 kg

MATURATION: 3 to 12 months

PRESENTATION: wrapped in waxed canvas

Sage Derby, strongly coloured and flavoured by the herb (TOP LEFT). CENTRE: Dorset Blue Vinney. TOP RIGHT: portrait of Henry VIII, whose reign saw the democratisation of cheese.

DORSET BLUE VINNEY

Dorset Blue Vinney (or Vinny) is a genuine regional cheese made in the Sherbourne Valley. It is a hard cheese made from the skimmed milk of one or more milkings. The cream was reserved for making butter, an important aspect of local economy. As the cheese matures, little cracks form, and this is where the mould develops. The origin of the mould has been explained by horse harnesses being kept in the same place as the cheese while it matures, the bacteria on the leather contaminating the cheese. Maturing could last up to 12 months or even be extended to 18. This produced a cheese of proverbial hardness giving rise, in local parlance, to countless comparisons. The Blue

Vinney manufactured nowadays has a much higher fat content than most of its predecessors and conforms to current required standards of hygiene. Imitations of this cheese originating from outside Dorset are sometimes sold under the name Dorset Blue.

■ DORSET BLUE VINNEY (OR VINNY)

Cow's milk cheese (40 to 46% fat)

TYPE: blue mould, uncooked, hard to semi-hard, natural thick rind

SHAPE: round, 15 cm in diameter, 20.5 cm high

WEIGHT: 4.5 kg

MATURATION: up to 9 months

GLOUCESTER

The reign of Henry VIII marked the advent of democracy for cheeses. Following the dissolution of the monasteries, cheese-production became the work of farmers. And since quality no longer depended on the strict observance of monastic rules,

the growing number of dairies resulted in a host of regional cheese varieties. Records show that Gloucester cheese was known outside the county as early as the 8th century. There are two types of Gloucester: Single Gloucester, weighing 6-7 kg and made from a mixture of skimmed milk from the evening and unskimmed milk from the morning, lighter in texture and flavour but more succulent than Double; and Double Gloucester, almost twice as heavy as the Single, and golden coloured, made with the unskimmed milk of two milking sessions. Gloucester is still at the heart of an old folk festival that dates back to times unknown. It is reminiscent of certain pagan celebrations even though it seems to have blended in with Whitsuntide.

On Whit Monday, in the hamlet of Randwick, the cheeses are decorated with flowers and ribbons and paraded through the village streets to welcome the return of sunny weather and wish their herds health and prosperity. Formerly, they used to take them round the church before sharing them out among the parish. At Cooper's Hill, the cheeses are taken up to the top of the hill, then rolled down to the bottom. Eating the cheese afterwards is all part of the fun, especially for the children who build up a healthy appetite racing them down. This ritual also provided an astringent test of the strength of the handsome and polished rind, which would have to be strong enough to protect the cheese on its journeys across to Europe and America. The cheese-merchants further tested its robustness by jumping on it with both feet. If the rind cracked, they did not buy.

In the 1970s, Patrick Rance was still selling impeccable, succulent-textured and naturally-ripened Double Gloucester. Unfortunately, the effort involved in producing such a hard rind and the length of time taken to mature the cheeses proved too much, so the cheese-maker (who had revived this tradition) was forced to abandon it. These days, even farmouse-made

Gloucester cheese is wrapped in canvas. The plastic-wrapped industrially-produced version meanwhile is too highly-coloured and no longer bears any relation to the traditional cheeses. Recent changes in taste and fashion have called for cheese flavoured with herbs, garlic, berries or spices. For example, various Double Gloucesters are now to be found: COTSWOLD with onion or chives, WINDSOR with elderberries, and SHERWOOD with pickles. WALTON, made with walnuts, combines

the smoothness of Double Gloucester with the tangy creaminess of Stilton.

■ GLOUCESTER

Cow's milk cheese (48% fat)

TYPE: pressed, uncooked, semi-hard, rough, pale-yellow or orangy rind

SHAPE: round, 38 cm in diameter, 5.5 cm high for "Single", and 38 cm by 13 cm high for "Double"

WEIGHT: 6-7 kg for "Single", and 10-12 kg for "Double"

MATURATION: up to 6 months

PRESENTATION: small label over red-brown waxy coating; wrapped in canvas

LANCASHIRE

This regional cheese is eaten while soft and has long been made using raw milk from cows that graze in fields swept by salt-laden haze and spray from the sea.

Windsor Red Cheese, flavoured with elderberry wine (ABOVE). TOP CENTRE: industrially-produced Double Gloucester. BOTTOM: Victorian cowshed at Eastwood Manor Farm, East Harptree. FOLLOWING PAGES: the North Yorkshire Dales.

Real Lancashire, cylindrical in shape and wrapped in canvas (often waxed canvas), is made with unpasteurised milk (unlike the bulk of Lancashire cheese). The curds from two successive days are hand-kneaded and pressed, in canvas, many times. The cheese's aroma, flavour and crumbly texture become apparent after 3 weeks, and at 6 months, it bears comparison with Laguiole. Pasteurised versions of the cheese do not display these characteristics however. The worst such version is the so-called "Simple Acid" (which is made using the over-salted curds of a single milking).There are also Lancashires with walnuts or sage which are mixed in with the curds.

Lancashire (BOTTOM) and Leicester (CENTRE). TOP RIGHT: Roche Abbey, Yorkshire.

■ LANCASHIRE

Cow's milk cheese (48% fat)

TYPE: pressed, uncooked, semi-hard

SHAPE: round, 30 cm in diameter, 25 cm high

WEIGHT: approx. 20 kg

MATURATION: 3 to 6 weeks

PRESENTATION: wrapped in waxed canvas, with a small label or band (not all the cheese is wrapped in canvas in this way however)

LEICESTER

Leicester used to be made in farms around Leicestershire, a major cheese-making region. It still is produced in this region but also nowadays by a few farmers and dairies outside the county using pasteurised milk. It is recognisable by its pronounced orangy-red colour. In earlier times, it was dyed by carrot juice, but for the past two hundred years it has been done using anatto.

■ LEICESTER

Pasteurised cow's milk cheese (48% fat)

TYPE: pressed, uncooked, semi-hard, natural rind

SHAPE: round, 30 or 50 cm in diameter, 12 cm high

WEIGHT: 9 or 20 kg

MATURATION: 3 to 6 months

STILTON

The king of English cheeses. Its name comes from the village of Stilton in Cambridgeshire on the old London-to-York road. Its was first sold in about 1720. According to tradition, a certain Elizabeth Scarbrow, housekeeper for the Ashby family living at Quenby Hall near Leicester, was the pioneer who invented Stilton. Both she and her daughter, Mrs Paulet, contributed towards its growth by supplying quality cheese to the Bell Inn, run by the latter's husband in Stilton. This coaching-house was soon to become famous. Towards the end of the 17th century, quite a number of farmers' wives were making Stilton from the first milk of the day. Daniel Defoe, author of *Robinson Crusoe*, stopped in Stilton during his various travels and was to look back at this village "renowned for its cheese" with fond memories. Shortly afterwards in 1733, the great poet, Alexander Pope, published his *Imitations of Horace*. In it, he devoted some of his verse to this already-famous cheese: "Cheese, such as men in Suffolk make But wish'd it Stilton for his sake". Stilton reached the peak of its glory when it formed a holy alliance with wines from the south. Who it was that first thought of gorging Stilton with port or Madeira using little metal tubes, nobody knows, but the marriage of rich Leicestershire meadow with fat, sun-swollen grapes from the Iberian peninsula was a happy one. After one week steeping in the wine, the rind is cut from the top and the cheese eaten by the spoonful. To close on a sombre note, COTTENHAM, a blue cheese close to Stilton, once manufactured in the Cambridge area, now no longer exists.

■ STILTON

Unskimmed cow's milk cheese
(48 to 55% fat, enriched with cream)
TYPE: blue mould, natural rind

SHAPE: round 20 to 30 cm in diameter,
40 cm high (large), or 25 cm high (small)
WEIGHT: 2 to 4.5 kg
MATURATION: from 6 to 12 months
in humid atmosphere

WENSLEYDALE

Although Blue Wensleydale has been around for several centuries, the white version has only existed for some hundred years. Originally a sheep's cheese, Wensleydale, from the Ure Valley in Yorkshire, is now made from cow's milk in Hawes and Kirkby Malzeard in the Ure Valley, also known as Wensleydale. Moving east-north-east, we meet SWALEDALE from the Swale Valley and COTHERSTONE from the Tees Valley in Durham. The two are only made on a very local level on small farms. An organic

Wensleydale is made in Otterbury in Northumbria, using unpasteurised cow's (Ayrshire) and sheep's (Friesland) milk. For a taste of some of the best locally-made farm products, try a slice of Wensleydale with a piece of apple tart.

■ WENSLEYDALE

Cow's milk cheese (48% fat)
TYPE: pressed, uncooked, semi-hard, white, or blue-veined for Blue Wensleydale; natural rind
SHAPE: round
WEIGHT: 1.2 or 5 kg

*H*arvest Supper
by Edna Bizon (LEFT).
BOTTOM LEFT: Stilton.
BOTTOM RIGHT: Blue Wensleydale.
BELOW: Farmhouse Wensleydale.

MATURATION: 4 weeks to many months

PRESENTATION: brand label on the rind

OTHER CHEESES

Cottage Cheese was the traditional fare for poor country folk. It is a soft, fresh curd made with skimmed milk and may also be eaten with fresh cream. In Scotland, they call it CROWDIE. CABOC (whose origins go back to the 15th century) is closer to butter in consistency and coated with oat flakes. LANARK BLUE sheep's milk cheese, DUNSYRE BLUE Ayrshire cow's milk cheese and bloomy BONCHESTER, are all made from unpasteurised milk and merit a mention. There is a whole range of organic farms in Wales producing cheeses made with unpasteurised milk. These include CAERPHILLY (MAESLLYN), LLANBOIDY, LLANGLOFFAN, PANT-Y-LLYN, TYNLGRUG, PENCARREG and CARDIGAN cheeses in county Dyfedd, and MARIANGLAS (goat's cheese) in Gwent.
From the north of England, CUMBERLAND

A typical Scottish Highlands cow (TOP). BOTTOM LEFT: Cottage Cheese. BOTTOM RIGHT: Milleens cheese from County Cork.

FARMHOUSE cheese (organic unpasteurised) and STAFFORDSHIRE cheese could also be mentioned. BEENLEIGH BLUE (organic sheep's milk cheese) from the South West is one of the best known of the new wave of sheep's and goat's milk cheeses. DUNLOP was invented, according to the legend, by Barbara Gilmour, in 1688. This softish, mild cheese is made from the milk of Ayrshire cattle. The Scots eat it relatively unmatured, but let it age longer for selling in other parts of the country or export abroad. This cheese is no longer made outside industrial dairies.
The Highlands and Islands of Scotland produce other mild farmhouse cheeses such as ORKNEY, a soft cheese with a natural rind which becomes pungent after a few weeks (no prizes for guessing where that comes from), and ISLAY from the Hebrides.

This relatively level land with its low relief has an oceanic climate and astoundingly little thermal variation (barely 10° C). Hence, the extreme mildness of its winters differs little from its cool summers. The rainfall, combined with its moderate temperature, is a blessing for plants. Even palm trees grow in the south of the country. The quality of its pasture explains why three quarters of Ireland's farming revenue comes from livestock. But, here as elsewhere, the number of farms is decreasing and little by little the smaller ones are disappearing. Ireland used to produce a wide range of local cheeses. Many of them have succumbed to the pressures of agricultural modernisation. Among those that fell by the wayside are MULCHAN – made from buttermilk, GRUS – a pressed cheese with a distinctive flavour, mild MILLSEN, and FAISCRE GROTHA – a traditional soft farm-cheese. However, at the end of the seventies,

master cheese-makers decided to promote produce no longer made outside their local areas. Similarly, to limit imports, Ireland began to make cheeses based on major cheeses of the world. And far from being pale imitations, thanks to quality methods and pasture, they are often quite novel or unusual. MILLEENS from County Cork is known throughout Ireland. It is a mild, washed-rind cheese, flat and round, and weighs some 1,5 kg. RYEFIELD, a small cheese coated in a black film, is a very mature Cheddar at heart. COOLEENEY, a very soft cheese, has quite a distinct flavour to it (farm-made Cooleeney is milder). GUBBEEN from the Cork area is a semi-hard, washed-rind cheese (there is also another variety, smoked over an oak fire). KERRY, manufactured in its namesake's county, is a semi-hard

cheese about 15 cm wide, and sometimes coated in wax. CORLEGGY, a goat's milk hard cheese with a natural rind, contains only non-animal rennet to cater for a vegetarian clientele. RING is a cylindrical cheese about 12 cm across and has the texture of a well-matured Gouda. The slightly tangy DESMOND tastes rather like the French Saint Nectaire, and GABRIEL which has holes like a Swiss cheese can be matured to full hardness. BAYLOUGH is a real local cheese with a well-defined taste. BALLYDAGUE is used in a number of recipes, while KNOCKANOUR resembles Port-Salut. Blue cheeses are produced in various parts of Ireland. County Cork is the home of CHETWYND BLUE, a cheese made from pasteurised cow's milk, and from Tipperary comes CASHEL BLUE, a mild cheese with

a rather lumpy texture. There are also cheeses made from sheep's milk, such as the 3 kg CRATLOE, as there are from goat's milk. Among the latter is the semi-hard LOUGH CAUM or CROGHAN. As in other places, Cheddar is also a major cheese because of its easy manufacturing process.

BLARNEY

This is the only old, typically-Irish cheese to be produced in large quantities. It is a semi-hard, cow's milk cheese with less than 50% fat. Although it's often called the Irish Gruyère because of its holes, it is actually closer to the Danish cheese Samsø.

■ BLARNEY

Cow's milk cheese (50% fat)

TYPE: semi-hard, reddish colour; hard rind

SHAPE: round

WEIGHT: approx. 10 kg

Farmers crossing the beach at low tide with the day's milk, Ballyferriter, Kerry (TOP). BELOW: view of the Glendalough valley, County Wicklow, Ireland.

Old-fashioned carved wooden milk churn (TOP RIGHT).
BOTTOM: the sulphur springs at Namaskar, near Myvatn, Iceland.
BELOW: Skyr.

Although the first people to set foot on Icelandic soil were almost certainly Irish monks, it was the Norwegian Vikings who, from 870 AD onwards, began colonising the "land of fire and ice" in any lasting manner. Present-day Icelandic is still very similar to old Norse, the vernacular these medieval settlers used to write the sagas. As well as fishing and hunting seals, the Vikings also planted crops and raised livestock on their slender strips of coastal land. The herds would roam freely throughout the summer and be herded into vast stone-walled enclosures, called *rettir,* in the autumn. They spent the winter in buildings that looked like traditional houses, covered in earth and grass, and which are now lovingly conserved. Later on, sturdy

Norwegian cattle were brought over, in turn followed by Danish cattle. Although less robust, these were better able to endure the long winter months in stables. Icelandic milk is renowned for its taste and purity, due to the quality of grass on this as yet unpolluted volcanic island. Because of its taste, the copies of Edam (BRAUDOSTUR), Tilsit (TILSITTER), Emmental (ODALOSTUR), Denmark's Havarti (BURI), or Camembert, Port-Salut and Brie (DALA-BRIE), made here all have a distinctive flavour.

SKYR

Along with dried or smoked fish, Skyr was and remains an everyday foodstuff. Originally, this soft white cheese was made without rennet: the milk was first warmed, then curdled by adding some

of the previous day's Skyr to it. The curds were then cut up into pieces and strained. Using rennet improved the cheese's quality but, even so, this simple manufacturing method is still used. Nowadays, Skyr is made from the whey of cow's milk used for making butter. Other derivatives of heated and reduced cow's milk whey include MYSINGUR and MYSUOSTUR, a brown, more or less malleable cheese rich in cream. Skyr is made and marketed in various forms: natural Skyr, Skyr with fruit: AVAXTSKYR, or with added cream: RJOMASKYR. And if there is anything left over after cheese-making, the rest is made into a drink, Mysa.

■ SKYR

Whey-based pasteurised cow's milk cheese (less than 10% fat)

TYPE: soft

MATURATION: eaten while fresh

PRESENTATION: 1-litre containers

In the past, poverty was the rule in this country and the size of the herd was limited by the land available to graze it on and the number of male or female members of the family there were to look after it (the long winters meant that greater amounts of fodder needed to be stored). Goats, which eat roots and grass on all manner of terrain, provided a bit of extra milk for the family and children. Nevertheless, with wild berries rich in vitamin C, eggs and cod's liver oil (whose bitter benefits Viking offspring were among the first to test), the Norseman's food was well-balanced in vitamins. So the terror inspired by these fighting-men, so full of energy and afraid of neither sword nor ice, should come as no surprise. Shortages at home incited them to sail over the seas to trade, selling amber, skins and fish and bringing back booty or slaves. The Viking epic lasted over two centuries. When they quietened down, having taken the best lands and married the daughters of their conquered foes, these ferocious fighters became honest farmers once more. They embraced the Christian religion preached by monks who still remembered the horrifying tales of their predecessors. These daring missionaries, often Irish monks,

had never hesitated to face storm and shipwreck to go and convert the worshippers of Thor and Odin at best, or, at worst, earn a martyr's death. Armed with cross and Bible, they brought another message with them for staving off the hunger that goaded the Norsemen on to foreign lands: "Preserve your milk". In other words, they taught them how to make cheese. The Scandinavians opted for the rather

more down-to-earth advantages of farming and soft cheeses instead of the hypothetical Valhalla of the Valkyries. With its long strip of seaboard facing the Norwegian Sea, Norway has an oceanic climate, attenuated by the presence of the Gulf Stream, and its steep mountains are regularly washed by heavy rainfall. Any grazing-land available is of good quality, but covers only some 0.3% of the total area; arable land is slightly more extensive: 3%. One quarter of the country is covered in forest, and the rest consists of mountains and, in the north, tundra. Waterlogged throughout the summer, in winter the tundra becomes a paradise for Lapps (or Saam) with their sledges and reindeer. Across the whole of Lapland, the inhabitants derive substantial income from these animals.

Wooden butter mould (diameter 20 cm). The inside of the lid is carved in relief which serves to imprint the butter with a "trademark". Top CENTRE: Norway produces more goat's milk than cow's milk. BOTTOM: Narvik Fjord, Norway.

A few of them, castrated males, are used for transport, while the rest are reared for their meat, which is much appreciated by people in the south. The Lapps make traditional cheeses from reindeer milk, as they do in Finland. Even though four inhabitants out of five live in towns today, city-dwellers never forget their ancestors were country-folk. The younger generations revere the simple wooden artefacts peasants of old used to use as household utensils. Pride of place among these symbols of time past are the pails once used for transporting milk, and the churns for making butter.

In the same way as the people living in the mountain regions, the peasants living in the interior also learned how to preserve their dairy products by transforming the by-products of milk (buttermilk) and cheese itself (whey) into more cheese. The results of this are the "fatless" cheeses – Gammelost

The milk of the female reindeer has a higher fat content than almost any other milk. It is used to make a few rare cheeses in Lapland, Norway and Sweden (BELOW). TOP: a sheep from the Voss region. BOTTOM RIGHT: Gammelost.

at 3% fat and Mysost – particularly sought after today for their low fat content. Spicy, sharp and smooth, they express the grim harshness of this country whose nature is as out of proportion as its breakfasts. Just look at one of their famous *frukosts* and see: spiced herrings immediately on waking, accompanied by miscellaneous cheeses, eggs and jam.

GAMMELOST

Gammelost is a traditional, strong-flavoured cheese manufactured around the sheer rock-faces and pastures towering over some of Norway's most spectacular fjords in the region of Bergen. Sognefjord (200 km long) is home to a sort of Gammelost made from goat's cheese, while Hardangerfjord (170 km long) produces one using cow's milk. The latter's name seems appropriate *(gammel* = old, and *ost* = cheese) because its natural

rind, created by the spontaneous bloom of greeny-brown mould, soon takes on the appearance of a ripe old cheese aged by time. Nonetheless, it may be eaten either young – after 1 month, or after 6 months or more. It is a question of personal taste.

For the lover of heady sensations, the maturing-process is completed by wrapping the Gammelost in straw macerated in gin. In this way, it can then pursue its slow internal ripening without running the risk of being attacked by undesirable insects or bacteria. And just as the English sometimes help their Stilton down with a good dose of port, so the Norwegians make their respectably-aged Gammelost somewhat more user-friendly by digging a hole with a knife or teaspoon and pouring in their favourite spirit: gin, aquavit or beer. And since we're in Scandinavia, the person driving the others home can always drink tea or coffee instead!

■ GAMMELOST

Goat's milk (Sognefjord) or cow's milk

(Hardangerfjord) cheese

TYPE: soft, blue mould. When very ripe,

the cheese becomes as hard

as Parmesan

SHAPE: round, sometimes rectangular

WEIGHT: 3 kg, sometimes more

MATURATION: 1 to 6 months and more

GJETOST

This is the country's most popular
cheese. Similar versions sold under
other names exist in other countries,
such as Getost in Sweden. In keeping
with the peasant tradition of home-
made cheese, it is made with whatever
is available, either cow's or goat's milk,
or both mixed together (the proportions
used today are 90% cow's milk and
10% goat's). Purists refuse to call
it cheese since, as they rightly claim,
it contains no rennet.

Nonetheless, Gjetost has fed generation
after generation of peasants and was
one of the many foodstuffs the Vikings
took with them on their various
expeditions. It is made using whey,
or *mysost* as it's called in Norwegian.
As its name suggests (*Gjet* = goat,
ost = cheese), it was originally a goat's
cheese, and only when it is made like

this can it be designated as authentic
(ekte). Consequently, if the only milk to
go into its manufacture is cow's milk, its
correct name is MYSOST. The whey left
over from making butter is heated gently
in stainless-steel vats. While it heats up,
it is stirred until it has reduced by three
quarters. This results in a brown caramel
paste called *prem*. Cream or milk are
added to increase the taste and fat
content, and then it is packed in slabs
ranging from 250 g to 1 kg.

PULTOST – which may also be named
after its region of production – is a low-
fat (10%) cow's milk cheese, also made
from whey. It can be processed similarly
to Gjetost by adding cream, spices
or aromatic herbs for extra flavour.

■ GJETOST

Goat's (ekte) or cow's milk cheese,

or mixture (35% fat)

TYPE: semi-hard and brownish

SHAPE: rectangular

WEIGHT: 250 g or 1 kg

PRESENTATION: wrapped in plastic

JARLSBERG

This ancient cheese, once all but
forgotten, was "re-instated" as a dairy-
farm cheese during the last century.
Jarlsberg, the "Emmental of the
Fjords", owes its name to the oldest
Viking establishment in Norway, close
to Tonsberg on the Oslofjord. It was
resurrected when some southern
farmers formed a cooperative in the
mid-19th century, and with the help of
the AS University's agricultural research
department. It uses the summer milk
from high-latitude pastures which,
due in part to the virtually continuous
northern sunshine, has very little
to envy the flora of Switzerland's alpine
pastures. Jarlsberg is a very popular
cheese in Norway, and is exported
to the United States and elsewhere.

Gjetost,
unwrapped (TOP),
and in its packaging
(ABOVE). BOTTOM:
Jarlsberg.

■ JARLSBERG

Pasteurised cow's milk cheese (45% fat)

TYPE: pressed, cooked, irregular spherical

holes; smooth rind

SHAPE: round, 30 cm in diameter, 10 cm high

WEIGHT: 10 kg

PRESENTATION: printed straight onto rind

Nökkelost (RIGHT).
BOTTOM: a shepherd
family in Delecarlie,
Sweden. 19th-century
painting. *Bibliothèque
des Arts Décoratifs,
Paris.*

NÖKKELOST

The Scandinavians brought various semi-hard cheeses back from Holland, such as Norbo and Ridder. Another of these was Nökkelost, a cheese containing cloves. In the 17th century, the Dutch town of Leyden had a monopolistic control over spices in western Europe. As a result Nökkelost now bears the keys to this city stamped on its rind (*nökkel* = keys).

■ NÖKKELOST

Cow's milk cheese (45% fat)

TYPE: pressed, uncooked, containing cloves, smooth rind

SHAPE: round or rectangular

WEIGHT: 5 to 15 kg

MATURATION: 3 months

PRESENTATION: labelled as is

This country has a long history of conquest behind it, and one that could by no means be called shy and withdrawn. Who could dismiss the vast European destiny of the Langobards, Burgundians and Goths descended from the ancient homelands of the Suiones? This Germanic tribe, mentioned in the 2nd century by the Roman historian Tacitus, gave rise to the modern name of Sweden. It is certainly difficult to assess the influence they had in terms of agriculture, but it should not be forgotten that the Burgundians gave their name to the French province of Burgundy, home to a remarkable variety of delicious cheeses and famous wines. The astounding transformation of pagan, war-mongering, conquering Vikings into peaceful farmers attached to their land was brought about by monks as convinced of their faith as their converts were of their own strength. In the 9th century, Charlemagne's son, Louis I, King of the Franks, sent the Benedictine missionary Anskar to Scandinavia. After a series of journeys to Jutland, from which he returned with his tail between his legs, Anskar eventually had better luck with the Swedes who authorised the opening of churches and the baptism of King Olaf by the Archbishop of York. Along with evangelisation, faith and holy books, the monks brought cheese-making manuals with them. In this rugged and hostile environment, they still needed to feed the temporal as much as the spiritual. As they set up

crosses in the land of Thor and Odin, they also built self-contained Cistercian monasteries with diary, fields and pasture. In time, the peasants living on this land were to pay their dues in dairy products, as was the case in other European countries.

As in Norway, the whey remaining from the butter and cheese intended for sale was always used. It was made into low-fat, caramel-coloured cheeses: GETOST, MESOST and GETMESOST. These cheeses, home-made for family consumption, are still traditional in Sweden. GOTAOST, or Gotland cheese, has been made from either cow's or goat's milk since time immemorial. Gotland, an island in the Baltic Sea, was a rallying-point for many a large-scale invasion and one of the major centres of Viking culture. Evidence

of Gotland's past glory can be seen in its rich burial-mounds, containing gold coins from across Europe. PRÄSTOST, a home-made soft cheese which undergoes a series of processing treatments, is a survivor of a long-dead custom. Otherwise known as "Priest's cheese" or "Presbytery cheese" (*präst* = priest), Prästost used to be made by the pastor's wife with the milk brought her by the parishioners. She first clotted the fresh milk, then salted it

and wrapped it in a cloth which she squeezed in order to speed up the draining-process. The cheese then spent the next few days in a cellar while it matured. Finally, it could be taken to market. It was made in a round shape and its weight varied according to the amount of milk available. It was also a means of gauging the generosity of the pastor's flock. A popular priest could reckon on selling cheeses weighing well over 10 kilos. Prästost now includes a number of profane varieties such as the SAALAND PFARR. The technique involves mixing a little whisky with the curds,

then washing the Prästost in whisky twice a week during maturation. All of this is done in a cool, humid cellar. Its flavour is not so very different from the French cheese, Langres au Marc de Bourgogne, a washed-rind cheese soaked in marc, a wine spirit made from the solid grape-remains after fermentation is completed.

ADELOST

The Swedes don't always go for the tangy cheeses, they are also great lovers of blue moulds. Adelost is a good example of this. It is industrially manufactured from cow's milk and shaped like a broad cylinder.

■ ADELOST

Pasteurised cow's milk cheese (45% fat)

TYPE: blue mould; natural rind

SHAPE: round, 18 cm in diameter, 10 cm high

WEIGHT: 2.5 kg

MATURATION: 2 to 3 months

PRESENTATION: wrapped in silver paper

HERRGÅRDOST

Sweden does produce a cheese of the Emmental type which is nevertheless a local product. And the Swedes make no mistake about it: they love it.

Typical farmhouse near the Danish border (TOP LEFT). CENTRE: Prästost. ABOVE: Åseda.

Although it is a semi-hard pressed cheese, it is slightly firmer than others of the same type. Its fat content is 45%, and though its holes might not be as big as those of Emmental, its flavour is as mild as its Swiss counterpart. Herrgårdost is wheel-shaped and takes about 3 months to reach maturity, but it can also be eaten when harder. GREVE is another wheel-shaped cheese and weighs about 15 kg or so, with a fat content in the region of 30 to 45%. Also like Emmental, it is renowned for its mildness, but it takes about 10 months to reach full maturity.

Caraway-flavoured
Kryddost (ABOVE).
TOP RIGHT: Sveciaost.
BELOW: Herrgårdost.

■ HERRGÅRDOST

Pasteurised medium-fat cow's milk

cheese for everyday consumption

(30 to 45% fat)

TYPE: pressed, heated (45° C), semi-hard

with holes; natural rind

SHAPE: round

WEIGHT: 12 to 20 kg

MATURATION: 4 months

PRESENTATION: labelled as is

HUSHÅLLSOST

It took Sweden quite a while before deciding to make a cheese from "unskimmed milk" since, traditionally, butter was first made for sale or export and what was left over was then used for cheese. Nowadays, Swedish dairies are backed up by highly efficient farming techniques and are provided with large amounts of high-quality milk – 5000 kg milk per cow per year! Based on a cooperative system tried and tested for over a century, they make excellent copies of big-name foreign cheeses: Cheddar, Gouda, Tilsit, Camembert, Brie and Port-Salut. But there is one local cheese they produce in the traditional peasant way: Hushållsost, a small, cow's milk cheese which sometimes contains as much as 60% fat. It is a pressed, uncooked cheese of cylindrical shape and fairly fast maturation: 2 months in a humid cellar.

■ HUSHÅLLSOST

Pasteurised cow's milk cheese

(up to 60% fat)

TYPE: pressed, uncooked, semi-hard;

natural rind

SHAPE: round

WEIGHT: 1 to 2 kg

MATURATION: 2 months

PRESENTATION: labelled as is

SVECIAOST

Sweden has long been an exporter of dairy products due to the development of Hanseatic trade: Novgorod, Riga, Visby, Danzig, Lübeck, Hamburg, Cologne, Bruges, London and Bergen. Commercial exchange between the Baltic and North Seas had major consequences for the spread of cheese-making techniques. The influence of the Netherlands, which had been suppliers of semi-hard cheeses for many years, can be judged by the number of Gouda and Edam type cheeses made here. One of these is Svecia, a respectably-sized cheese with a waxed rind weighing 20 kilos. It is a pressed, semi-hard cheese with a fat content of 45% and little holes. It is eaten at various stages of ripening depending upon whether it is preferred mild (3 months) or strong (1 year or over). There are varieties of Svecia coated in red wax flavoured with either caraway or cloves. Both of these may be eaten after a short maturation of only 8 weeks. VÅSTERBOTTEN is a close cousin to Svecia but larger. It is a flattish round cheese, pressed, uncooked and has a short maturation period (from 8 to 10 weeks), and hence a milder taste. Those who prefer strong, sharp cheeses however, are of course entirely free to eat it in a riper state. KRYDDOST, another cylindrical, caraway- or cloves-based cheese is a typical example of a sharp-tasting cheese to be eaten "old" (12 months or more). There is a large number of faster-maturing cheeses containing spices (caraway, cloves or pepper) in varying amounts. Of the same type is RIDDAROST, a rindless cheese, with or without spices, that finishes its maturation process in its final packaging.

■ SVECIAOST

Pasteurised cow's milk cheese
(30-50% fat)

TYPE: pressed, uncooked, semi-hard; waxed rind

SHAPE: round, approx. 30 cm in diameter, 13 cm high

WEIGHT: 12 to 14 kg

MATURATION: 2 to 4 months or more

PRESENTATION: stamped as is

Many thousands of years ago, the Finns came from the vast steppes west of the Urals and learned cattle-farming, and other ways of using milk, from their Baltic neighbours. Despite the continental climate, Finnish cows are far from being able to spend all year outdoors in lush green meadows like most of their kith and kine. The rigorous conditions of such high latitudes mean farmers have to keep their animals warm in stables throughout the six months of icy winter. Finland was annexed to Sweden for quite a lengthy period, during which time they were also in contact with western cheese-making techniques. Although traditional cheese is still made in the countryside, in the Baltic ports foreign cheese from the west has long been more common. It is as if Finnish eyes have been looking westwards ever since the Middle Ages. The American author, D S Connery, has described Finland as "the eccentric man of Europe", and although it may well be in terms of its geography, language and history – it has lost over fifty wars with Russia, but still managed to remain independent – it certainly is where its cheeses are concerned: they are like no other. In the land of the Aurora Borealis, the

vast northern expanses beyond the Arctic Circle, reindeer cheese is as popular as its meat. Reindeer cheese is a speciality which, as could almost be expected in these freezing-cold arctic regions, is dunked in hot coffee. To make it, milk is warmed to 38° C and rennet added to produce curds which are then pressed, cut up into rectangular slabs and dried. Farmers still enjoy making local cheeses; one of these is called ILVES, a two-pound cheese with a maximum fat content of 45% to which they add an egg during the clotting. Nowadays, more Ilves is produced industrially than on the farm or in the

Finnish Gruyère being made in Tenala (TOP). BELOW: a Finnish landscape.

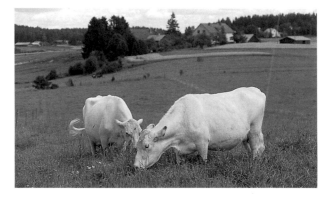

A Finnish peasant-woman holding a Juustoleipa cheese over the flames in the grate (RIGHT). BELOW: Finnish Gruyère.

BOTTOM: an assortment of Finnish cheeses: at the back, Tutunmaa, in the centre, Ilves, and to its left, Juustoleipa. FAR RIGHT: an old Danish forge in Orbach, Fionie.

home. Another cheese, JUUSTOLEIPA, undergoes the painful experience of being grilled in front of a nice hot fire before being allowed to mature.

The state of dilapidation the country found itself in at the end of the Second World War and the exorbitant war damages it had to pay to the USSR in record time literally forced Finland to equip itself with an ultramodern industry in order to survive. But starting from scratch does have one advantage: all the latest machines and technology. Finland, like its other Scandinavian neighbours, has sought to increase its agricultural output, quality and efficiency by adopting the cooperative

method. Swiss cheese-makers have been called in to teach the Finns how to make Emmental. Today, the bulk of all Emmental exported to the United States comes from Finland.

TUTUNMAA

The land of a thousand lakes prides itself on its completely pollution-free nature and produces a broad range of cheeses with unmistakably Finnish names, for both the domestic and export markets. Nowadays, everything is automated in the dairy industry and the level of hygiene is typical of "Scandinavian quality" standards. Tutunmaa is one of the various pasteurised cheeses of the Gouda type. And its taste certainly owes something to the excellent pastures its cows are put out to graze on. Other Gouda type cheeses include KARTANO and KORSHOLM. But Finland also makes Cheddar, which they call JUHLA, Tilsit, named KREIM, and a blue, Roquefort type cheese called AURA.

■ TUTUNMAA

Pasteurised cow's milk cheese (50% fat)

TYPE: pressed, uncooked, semi-hard, with small, irregular holes; natural, waxed rind

SHAPE: round

WEIGHT: 6 kg (10 kg for Korsholm)

MATURATION: 2 to 3 months

Four thousand years ago, the Danes were already big drinkers of milk. They did not make cheese as we understand it today, i.e. by using rennet, but they did allow the milk to turn somewhat and become acid, which could be described as a step in the right direction. Crop-farming, stock-breeding and trade began to flower when the climate started to warm up in around 1500 BC. This, in the strictest sense of the term, was the Golden Age of Scandinavia. Although these people had no gold, no copper and no tin, they soon became some of the most accomplished

goldsmiths in Europe. As they were in control of the amber trade-route in the Baltic, the metals could be obtained through bartering southwards with neighbouring tribes. A thousand years later, when cooler temperatures reduced the cereal harvests, the farmers had to build stables to shelter their animals, and take in enormous stores of hay to last the now long winters.

Moving on to the 9th century, we find extensively-wooded country but little soil on which to sow crops. This was the catalyst behind the expeditions of the land-hungry Scandinavians. The Danish Vikings found what they were looking for in Normandy, where land and climate reminded them of home. While its northern neighbours, shivering from their "polar winters" in mountainous and often arid regions, delight in their harsh yet spectacular environment, Denmark, whose highest peak is less than 200 metres, thanks heaven for the mild and rainy oceanic climate that bathes its immense string of island meadows stretching from Germany to Sweden.

In the 13th century, growth in towns and trade stimulated the country's economy and enabled a part of its

wares to be exported. "Dutch cheeses" became a popular merchandise, partly because of taste and partly because of necessity: they travel well. Then as now, cheeses were subject to strict manufacturing rules; as well as being symbols of social success.

To demonstrate their prosperity and impress people, farmers competed to produce the largest cheeses. Changes in land-ownership status, a sense of insecurity and small farmers refusing to acknowledge their social condition have never been ideal companions for progress in the cheese industry. Following a number of conflicts between Denmark and Sweden from the 16th century onwards, the peasants began to feel oppressed by the increasing obligations towards their lords. But the situation worsened,

and they fell into the clutches of land-owners or immigrant Germans. At this point, there were less than one thousand independent farmers. It was not until 1788 that new laws made it possible for land to be redistributed. The mid-19th century heralded the end of royal absolutism and, in the early years of the 20th century, the cooperative movement came to power, as did individual decision-making and the boom years for cheese-making.

DANABLU

Having made Dutch-type cheeses for centuries, Denmark began to look at cheeses from further south. Roquefort, Gorgonzola and other blue cheeses came under the inquisitive eye

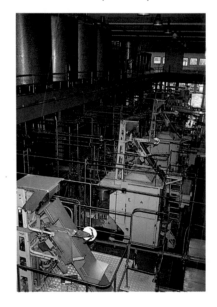

View of a canal in Copenhagen (TOP). BOTTOM: inside a contemporary Danish dairy factory.

Mycella (ABOVE).
TOP: Danablu.
FAR RIGHT: Danbo.
BOTTOM: a colourful
Faroe Islands harbour.

of Danish cheese-makers. Obviously, they could not imitate them perfectly, but the quality of Danish pasture and the continuous quality control imposed by the industry created Danish blue cheeses with their own special qualities. Danablu, or MARMORA, much appreciated at home, is a runaway success abroad. Shaped like a Roquefort and made from homogenised cow's milk, it is pale with blue-green veins and comes wrapped in silver paper printed with the brand-name. MYCELLA is another Danish blue cheese, but creamier. It is to Gorgonzola what Danablu is to Roquefort. Seeded with *Penicillium mycellium,* which gives it greener veins, it is a larger cheese than Danablu, weighing from 5 to 9 kilos.

■ DANABLU

Pasteurised cow's milk cheese

(50 to 60% fat), protected by

the Stresa Convention

TYPE: blue mould, yellowish rind

with mould

SHAPE: round, 20 cm in diameter

WEIGHT: 3 kg for round cheeses,

2 kg or more for slabs

MATURATION: 2 to 3 months

PRESENTATION: wrapped in silver paper

printed with the brand

DANBO

Danbo is a semi-hard cheese related to Samsø with regular holes of average size. It is shaped like a thick slab and sometimes contains caraway seeds. It is one of the country's major cheeses, being one of the best loved and biggest selling. FYNBO, ELBO, SVENBO and MOLBO are all similar to it in their texture and slightly aromatic flavour.

TYBO was created in a little village in the north of the island of Sjælland and is one of Denmark's oldest cheeses. Both with and without spices, it has been imitated and named after various regions. The Danes turned Tybo into a famous cheese abroad when Christian II (1513-1523)

called in Dutch cheese-makers to act as "technical consultants". MARIBO, coated in a film of pale yellow wax, is a distant cousin to Gouda. It is a pressed, semi-hard cheese with a fairly strong flavour and a number of irregular-shaped little cavities. Sold in both round and square shapes of 9 to 14 kg, it contains 30 to 45% fat, and is also available with caraway seeds.

■ DANBO

Pasteurised cow's milk cheese (45% fat)

TYPE: pressed, uncooked, semi-hard,

medium-sized holes, with or without

caraway; natural rind with yellowish wax

SHAPE: 25 cm slabs

WEIGHT: 6 kg

MATURATION: 2 to 3 months, plus washing

ESROM

This very mild cow's milk cheese takes its name from the ancient monastery of Esrom on the island of Sjælland. It was "rediscovered" by the Danish

Cheese Institute who made it conform to today's eating-habits.

■ ESROM

Pasteurised cow's milk cheese

(45 or 60% fat), protected by

the Stresa Convention of 1951

TYPE: pressed, malleable and fat with

irregular little holes, with or without

caraway or spices; thin rind

with yellow wax

SHAPE: slab

WEIGHT: 200 g to 2 kg

MATURATION: 3 weeks

PRESENTATION: wrapped in gold paper

printed with the brand

HAVARTI

This Danish speciality bears the name of the farm where the cheese was first perfected in the middle of the last century by a peasant-woman who travelled through Europe to study cheese-making techniques. Havarti is now one of the country's most famous

cheeses. It taste is more or less tangy according to the degree of maturation.

■ HAVARTI

Pasteurised cow's milk cheese

(30 or 45% fat)

TYPE: pressed, uncooked, semi-hard,

irregular little holes, with or without

herbs or spices; natural thin rind

sometimes coated with red wax

SHAPE: round or slab

WEIGHT: 2 to 4.5 kg

MATURATION: 1 month, washed rind

SAMSØ

In the early 19th century, the King of Denmark's interest in cheese and his determination to do as well in this area as elsewhere can be seen in his invitation to Swiss cheese-makers to come and teach their art. Having mastered the manufacturing processes, Danish farmers produced their own mild, semi-hard cheese with a hazelnut flavour, half way between Tybo and the

famous Swiss cheese with its big holes. Baptised with the name of an island in the Grand Belt, one of the straits controlling the entry to the Baltic Sea, Samsø has become the archetype of Danish cheeses. It has small holes and is often shaped like a Swiss cheese with a diameter of about 45 cm.

■ SAMSØ

Pasteurised cow's milk cheese (45% fat)

TYPE: pressed, semi-hard, little holes,

natural rind sometimes coated

with printed yellow wax

SHAPE: round, 45 cm in diameter

WEIGHT: approx. 14 kg

MATURATION: 3 to 6 months

Esrom (TOP LEFT).

CENTRE: Havarti.

ABOVE: Samsø.

BELOW: a typical house

with grass sown on

the roof. Elduvik,

Faroe Islands.

Frisian dairymaid
(ABOVE). Detail of
a 16th-century
watercolour.
BOTTOM: still-life with
cheese and ham
by van Schooten
(17th century).
OPPOSITE: the highly
renowned cheese
market at Alkmaar.

The major cheeses originating in the Netherlands can be counted on the fingers of one hand, but they have conquered the world so completely that innumerable copies and varieties of them now exist. Their ease of manufacture, smoothness and gastronomic qualities have made them very much in demand. Gouda, Edam and their derivatives often occupy first place in countries that have only recently developed a cheese-making industry. With more than half the land below sea-level, it is not surprising the Low-landers say that "God created the earth and left the Dutch to create Holland". The first people to inhabit the land have left many a sign of their constant battle against the encroaching water. Over a thousand years ago in Friesland, in the north of the country, they built large mounds – *terpens* – on top of which they built their wooden houses. Before the Romans arrived, the country was occupied by three peoples of Germanic origin: in the north, the Frisians had the coastal area; the Chamavi had Holland itself; and the Batavians had the mouths of the Rhine and Meuse. These different tribes reared cattle and made cheese of the simplest sort: fermented milk and soft white cheese. Among the various archaeological finds discovered in the remains of pre-Roman habitations were a number of cheese-draining vessels. The techniques of dyke-construction and canal-digging, which eventually led to the creation of the polders (literally, land reclaimed by dykes) now used as pasture, were introduced by the Romans who reached as far up as the Rhine. This vast river, which provided an excellent line of defence, set the northern limit to the Roman Empire. Demobilised Roman legionnaires settled and farmed the land but did not simply restrict themselves to growing cereal crops. It was in the common interest to develop the region so the Romans taught their vanquished local populations that the best way to preserve milk was to turn it into cheese, and especially, hard cheese. In the 5th century however, they began to succumb to invasions. Whereas the more or less Romanised Batavians did mix in with the Saxons, the Frisians remained firmly anchored in their dunes and put up a fierce resistance to the Saxons and Franks. They were at last put down by the Frankish invasion of Pepin II, whose illegitimate son Charles Martel was to expel the Arabs from France in the decisive battles of Tours and Poitiers in 732. It was Anglo-Saxon missionaries who finally won the day, with the foundation of the Archbishopric of Utrecht, Holland's religious centre, by the monk Willibrord in 695. The indomitable Frisians continued to resist on many occasions but they too ended up being annexed to the empire of Charlemagne, the father

FRANCE

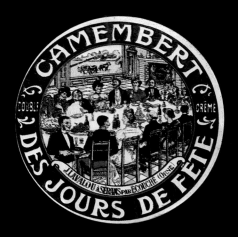

A cheese-maker overseeing the maturation of Munster cheeses (RIGHT), in the valley of the same name in Alsace.
CENTRE: Munster.
FAR RIGHT: caraway-flavoured Munster.
BELOW: labels for two other cheeses from this area; Petit Munster

and Carré de l'Est.
BOTTOM RIGHT: pastureland in the Vosges mountains, painted by J-F Millet.
OPPOSITE: Pavin, Carré de l'Est and, in front, Tamié.

the abbey but also the entire valley surrounding it. Munster constituted part of the rent that peasants paid to the local monks whose lands they cultivated. Subsequently, the cheese and the making of it spread into neighbouring areas, without however going further than the southern frontier between Alsace and the Franche-Comté.

This washed, penetratingly-scented cheese was made from Vosgian cows grazed in the valleys or on mountain pastures called *chaumes*. Today however, milk from such herds is scarcely ever used, even for farmhouse Munster, which has moreover become increasingly rare. Most production is now carried out in factories using pasteurised milk. Munster, whose strong odour and full-bodied flavour account for its originality and fame, has gained nothing from industrialisation, other than a greater availability to refined palates.

Munster, which Alsatians recommend should be eaten with warm jacket-

potatoes, has a cousin, GÉROMÉ, a cheese native to the small village of Gérardmer (pronounced Géromé) near Munster. Also known as MUNSTER DES VOSGES, this cheese is made by a process very similar to that of Munster itself, but it is thicker. Géromé is usually sold in a wooden box.

■ MUNSTER

Cow's milk cheese (farmhouse: raw milk; industrial: pasteurised) (50% fat)

TYPE: soft; washed (industrial) or bloomy (farmhouse)
SHAPE: round, 13 to 20 cm in diameter, 2.5 to 5 cm thick
MATURATION: 2 to 3 months for farmhouse Munster; sometimes finished in co-operative cellars; shorter ripening period for industrial Munster
PRESENTATION: as is, paper-wrapped, or boxed, with producer's label

Picodons from the Ardèche (BELOW), wrapped in sweet

chestnut leaves. BOTTOM: a farm near Pont-en-Royens in the Isère, formerly Dauphiné province. TOP RIGHT: small Banons. CENTRE RIGHT: Saint-Marcellins. OPPOSITE: southern cheeses: Tomme, small goat's cheeses, Banons and Picodons.

In the wake of its domination by the Voconces, the Allobroges, and the Romans, the ancient province of the Dauphiné was subjected to numerous partitions. And its goat, cow, and mixed cheeses are as disparate as the land, a region devoid of natural frontiers. While Savoie faces Switzerland and northern Italy, the Dauphiné turns the other way, spreading across the slopes of the Alpine massif towards Avignon and Haute-Provence. In the summer, the Chartreuse, Vercors, Champsaur and Queyrons are overrun by sheep driven up from Provence to graze on the tender grass found at higher altitudes. The milk from these animals is used to make cheese for local consumption. The Dauphiné produces small Tommes that bear the name of their mountain origins. There are also recently-created cheeses which mingle the milk of cows with that of goats.

PICODON

The Drôme's Picodon is a goat's cheese that shares AOC protection with Picodon of the Ardèche, on the opposite bank of the Rhône, and the Picodons of several neighbouring communes (Valréas in the Comtat Venaissin, Barjac in the Gard). Dieulefit, in the Drôme, at the same altitude as Montélimar, is the curing centre for the best-known Picodon. Best period: between May and June. Ardèche Picodon is ripened dry for a month, then washed with white wine or eau-de-vie and wrapped in a grape leaf.

■ PICODON

Goat's milk cheese (45% fat)

TYPE: soft; fine, bluish, natural rind, yellow-gold or red, depending on the degree of maturation

SHAPE: round, approximately 7 cm in diameter, 3 cm thick

WEIGHT: about 100 g

MATURATION: 1 month, dry

OTHER CHEESES

BANON is a goat's cheese from Banon in Haute-Provence. It is easily recognised by its wrapping of chestnut leaves tied with raffia string. Depending on the time of year, one also finds Banon made from the milk of sheep and cows. Soaked in eau-de-vie during its

ripening period, Banon finishes curing in its wrapping. The cheese can also be eaten fresh. Banon exists in several varieties, seasoned with spices or with savary, as in BANON AU POIVRE D'ANE (donkey's pepper), so called after the Provençale term for savary.

SAINT-MARCELLIN, which resembles a goat's cheese, is actually manufactured from cow's milk, but it can also be found made with goat's milk or with a mixture of the two, even at Saint-Marcellin itself. This sweet-tasting cheese is consumed either fresh or somewhat matured. The small TOMMES DE CHAMPSAUR and DE QUEYRÀS are sold in the local markets as well as in adjacent *départements*. The high Queyras valley produces a highly-esteemed blue cheese.

A vast mountain range of volcanic origin, France's Massif Central is covered with forests and pasturage of excellent quality, thanks to soil rich in phosphates, magnesium, and potassium. Only the chalky terrain of the Causses constitutes a poor soil, but even this adds to the cheese patrimony through its natural grottoes, which are perfect for ripening Roquefort. While presenting a certain geographical unity, the Massif Central is exposed to extremely diverse climates – oceanic and humid in the west, dry and cold in the east, and Mediterranean in the south – which are reflected in the region's great variety of farm produce, milk and cheese in particular. Unlike the Alps, the Massif Central is not cut through by great valleys that facilitate travel. Although the passes are not very high (culminating at 1,885 metres), their orientation makes communications difficult in winter. Still, most of this region was populated very early. The Celts, in particular the Arvernes who gave their name to the Auvergne, arrived around the 7th century BC and started clearing pastures and cultivating fields. In the 1st century BC, the Romans, Pliny in particular, were impressed by the quality of the local cheeses.

By the mid-19th century, the rather densely populated Massif Central was losing it inhabitants to the capital. Here again the railway played an important role by encouraging Auvergnats to go up to Paris, where they opened wood and coal businesses and, most of all, cafés-restaurants. This was how their native products became so well known abroad, their many cheeses first and foremost. Until recently, the menus of Parisian restaurants still listed Auvergnat and Normandy cheeses more often than Savoyard and Alsatian ones.

BLEU D'AUVERGNE

Another imitation Roquefort but made from cow's milk, Bleu d'Auvergne is also entitled to AOC protection. As its name suggests, the cheese comes from regions that once formed the old province of the Auvergne: the *départements* of Cantal, Puy-de-Dôme, Haute-Loire, Aveyron, Corrèze, Lot, and Lozère. It is made with milk from the famous Salers and Aubrac cows. *Penicillium glaucum* induces a blue-green veining well distributed throughout the cheese. Once cut, churned, and drained, the curds become cheese that is turned and then pierced by long needles laden with *Penicillium*, which grows in the passages left by the piercing. Next, the cheese is kneaded into moulds 20 cm in diameter, then drained. The cheeses are now left for a day or two at a temperature of 20° C. Depending on the size of the cheese, curing in a humid

The traditional Auvergnat "Bois et Charbons" (Wood and Coal) shop so familiar to Parisians. In the cafés adjoining these shops, customers were able to taste succulent cheeses, brought straight up from the Massif Central.
OPPOSITE: ram sculpted on a Romanesque capital in Roquefort-sur-Soulzon.

cellar with a maximum temperature of 10° C takes from 2 to 3 weeks. Every cheese is turned numerous times to remove the dampness. Finally it is wrapped in silver paper stamped with the producer's label and left to finish ripening in the buyer's cellar.

Bleu d'Auvergne has sparked off a pair of local derivatives: BLEU DE THIÉZAC and BLEU DE LAQUEUILLE. The latter came into being during the 19th century when a Laqueuille farmer also got the idea of inseminating his cheese with moulds from rye bread. All these blue cheeses are excellent from April to November.

The use of long needles to implant the *Penicillium* (TOP) will give the cheese its marbled character. RIGHT: Bleu d'Auvergne. BOTTOM: Bleu des Causses. FAR RIGHT: milk deliveries on the Causse. This mode of transportation is long-forgotten today, but it did have its charm and picturesque qualities. OPPOSITE: postcards of an Auvergnat dairy (TOP) and illustrating the "modern" method of making Cantal.

BLEU DES CAUSSES

The famous Roquefort inspired a blue cheese made from cow's milk, Bleu des Causses, which is produced in areas with richer pastures capable of feeding both cows and sheep. At one time it was made almost entirely in the Causses mountains. Sown with *Penicillium roqueforti*, the cheese is matured in caves ventilated by *fleurines*, just as Roquefort is in the Cambalou. These caves are called "bastard caves" because sheep's milk Roquefort is never ripened there, only the blue cheese made from cow's milk, albeit sometimes mixed with sheep's milk. As well as BLEU DU QUERCY, there is also

a cheese manufactured in a region of the Causses west of the Rouergue.

■ BLEU DES CAUSSES

Cow's milk cheese (45% fat)

TYPE: creamy blue-mould

SHAPE: round, 20 cm in diameter, 8 to 10 cm high

WEIGHT: 2.5 kg

MATURATION: about 2.5 months in a cool, humid cave

PRESENTATION: wrapped in foil and labelled

CANTAL

Probably one of the world's oldest cheeses, Cantal is also one of the best known of those made in the Auvergne. The Romans discovered and fell in love with it as soon as they conquered the region. Since then, Cantal has never ceased to make converts. Today, the cheese boasts an AOC, which limits its production to the *département* of the

■ BLEU D'AUVERGNE

Cow's milk cheese (45% fat)

TYPE: firm, creamy, and nicely-blue

SHAPE: round, 20 cm in diameter, 10 cm high; also available in half-size

WEIGHT: 1 to 2.5 kg

MATURATION: 3 months in a cool, humid cellar

PRESENTATION: wrapped in foil printed with the producer's label

LE CANTAL PITTORESQUE
1079. Riom-ès-Montagnes
Transport du Lait à la Fromagerie

L'AUVERGNE   Aujourd'hui   Autrefois

327 — **Fabrication du Fromage du Cantal**

Librairie Baudel, St-Céré (Lot)

A cross-section of the inside of a cellar used for maturing Roquefort (ABOVE). TOP RIGHT: the Roquefort cellars seen from the road. BELOW: the first *raclage*, or scraping, of the cheeses. Drawings from *Le Tour du Monde, 1875*. OPPOSITE: Old-fashioned wooden moulds and drainers for Fourme d'Ambert.

the shepherd happened to revisit the scene, where he found the food he had left still there, just inside the cave. Seized by hunger, he sank his teeth into the now solidified milk and, to his great surprise, found it delicious. Taking a closer look, he also noticed that the cheese was spangled with small blueish spots. With this, a young, smitten shepherd became the legendary inventor of a cheese that would travel the world over and honour the table of kings and emperors. The method for making the soft cheese from sheep's milk has been protected since 1411, when Charles VI signed a charter granting the inhabitants of Roquefort-sur-Soulzon a monopoly for the village's product. The law of 26th July, 1926, which for the first time gave AOC status to a cheese, virtually consecrated the "caves de Roquefort" – the natural grottoes of the Cambalou. Most of the milk used here comes from a

production area comprising several *départements:* Aveyron (representing three-quarters of the territory), Tarn, Lozère, Hérault, and Gard. Until 1985 however, this "native" milk might be complemented with some ready-curdled sheep's milk imported from Corsica or the Basses-Pyrénées. The variously-derived ingredients were carefully analysed and balanced so that once mingled they would constitute an entirely homogeneous raw material. Now, since the development of AOC-acknowledged products in both Corsica and the Pyrénées-Atlantiques, the cheese-makers of Roquefort have been obliged to find their auxiliary supplies elsewhere.

Roquefort-sur-Soulzon is in the Causses, a part of France whose name comes from the Latin *calx*, "chaux" in modern French or lime in English. The chalky, permeable soil is shot through with caves hollowed out by streaming water. The erosion has also created numerous cracks allowing the air to circulate. Laden with moisture and a special kind of mould, the *fleurines* or air currents, encourage the multiplication of *Penicillium roqueforti*, which in turn generate the blue-green veining that accounts for the tremendous reputation of the creamy,

delicately-flavoured and richly-aromatic Roquefort. First however, the milk is left to curdle for two hours in large vats, after which the curds are *sabré*, that is cut up into small cubes. This initial step is sometimes taken at the actual site of milk production. To obtain the *Penicillium*, a large loaf of yeast bread made with barley and rye is prepared and placed in the cave. Three months later the bread has grown a fine, furry coat, which, when dried and reduced to powder, is sprinkled on the curd-filled, drum-shaped cheese moulds. Later, one mould is placed upside-down on a second one so that fermentation will occur on the interior. Draining requires that the forms be turned several times a day. Next, the process of maturation begins in the vaulted caves, where it

lasts three months, during which time the cylindrical cheeses rest flat on oak planks. Finally, the ripened products are wrapped in foil and sent to market.

■ ROQUEFORT

Sheep's milk cheese (45% fat)

TYPE: creamy, blue-veined throughout

SHAPE: round, 19 to 20 cm in diameter, 8.5 to 10.5 high

WEIGHT: 2.5 kg (10 litres of milk)

MATURATION: 3 months in the humid caves of the Cambalou at 7° C

PRESENTATION: silver paper with the producer's label

SAINT-NECTAIRE

Saint-Nectaire is produced in the same region and with the same milk as Cantal. And the cheese may be equally old, although it did not acquire patents of nobility

Roquefort (TOP). FAR RIGHT: wiping the cheese. BELOW: detail from a 19th-century still-life: an artist's impression of Bleu d'Auvergne. OPPOSITE: carved wooden press and moulds. PRECEDING PAGES: the caves where Roquefort is matured.

until the Maréchal de Saint-Nectaire urged Louis XIV to taste it. Farmhouse Saint-Nectaire, which now accounts for less than half the production, is recognisable by its small green label. Nevertheless, be it farmhouse or dairy, the cheese has all the benefits of AOC designation. It originated south of Clermont-Ferrand in the Auvergne's Dore Mountains. Since the pastures blanketing these volcanic heights are at an altitude of 1000 metres, Saint-Nectaire evinces all the qualities of the mountain flora native to a world rich in thermal waters. However, such qualities do not always obtain in dairy-made Saint-Nectaire, which is manufactured with pasteurised milk sometimes taken from animals grazed on meadows treated with insecticides that have destroyed a number of plant species. Connoisseurs also regret the use of milk from Montbéliard cows, which are less adapted to volcanic soil than the local Salers and Clermont-Ferrand cows, whose milk is reserved for farmhouse Saint-Nectaire. Thanks to its modest dimensions, Saint-Nectaire can be produced on small farms. The cheese is made after every milking, morning and evening. Rennet must be introduced while the milk is still warm, after which coagulation takes an hour. The resulting

curds are broken into small grains, drained, freshly curdled, then poured into a mould and pressed. Once removed from the mould, the cheese is salted on both sides and pressed anew before being left to dry for two or three days. The subsequent cure gives Saint-Nectaire its pronounced, cavern-like aroma. Maturing generally takes place in old wine-cellars excavated in chill

volcanic rock (10° C). The wholesalers who own the caves buy the cheeses still "white" (fresh) from farmers or small manufacturers in order to ripen them for a month or two on a bed of rye straw. At the outset of this process, the Saint-Nectaires are frequently washed in brine. While hardening, the rind grows an all-over coat of white and grey mould. Once the rind has produced yellowish or reddish

"blooms" the cure is finally completed. PAVIN, named after a lake in the Auvergne near Saint-Nectaire, is a washed-rind cheese similar to creamery Saint-Nectaire in both taste and texture, but smaller (13 cm in diameter). MUROL, a recent creation named after the village in the Puy-de-Dôme from which it comes, is a more neutral flavoured derivative of Saint-Nectaire. The cheese is distinguishable by its orangy-red colour as well as by the hole bored out of its centre for the sake of an accelerated cure. The central core thus removed, called TROU DU MUROL or "Murol hole" is sealed in wax and marketed separately.

■ SAINT-NECTAIRE

Cow's milk cheese (45% fat)

TYPE: pressed, uncooked, semi-hard, pink or reddish, brine-washed rind

SHAPE: round, 12 cm in diameter, 3.5 cm thick

WEIGHT: 1.5 kg

MATURATION: 2 months in a cold, humid cellar

PRESENTATION: wrapped and labelled, a green circle signifying farmhouse Saint-Nectaire, a green square for dairy

OTHER CHEESES

In addition to the *grands crus,* or major cheeses, that make the reputation of the Massif Central, there are lesser cheeses in curious or interesting shapes and sizes. GAPERON, for example, is a product of *récupération,* or recovery, originally made with buttermilk seasoned with garlic and peppercorns. Thanks to its success, this cheese is now manufactured with whole or lightly skimmed milk (40% fat content). Semi-spherical in shape, Gaperon is tied with raffia, a reminder of poor peasants who used to ripen their cheeses by hanging them from the fireplace. It used to be said that the fortune of a young woman about to marry could be estimated by the number of Gaperons drying in her parents' house.

BRIQUE DU FOREZ, so called for its brick-like shape, is also known as CABRIOU or CABRION. As the name implies, it comes from the Forez region in the north-east part of the Massif Central. Although a goat's cheese, Brique du Forez sometimes contains cow's milk. Traditionally, it is made by cowherds in the same area that produces the famous Fourme d'Ambert. Some 12 cm long and 2.5 cm thick, Briques du Forez are ripened in 3 weeks. In the Ardèche and Cévennes, one finds PÉLARDONS, small farm-made goat's cheeses 6 to 7 cm in diameter, 2 to 3 cm thick. In the 1970s, these regions were invaded by young people "going back to the land" and who, very often, plunged into goat-cheese production. Present in abundance at the market in Anduze, at the gates to the Cévennes, and in the Languedoc, these little Pélardons are easy to prepare. They may be consumed at any stage in the curing process, which takes 2 or 3 weeks.

Murol (FAR LEFT). TOP: Saint-Nectaire. BOTTOM: Pavin. OPPOSITE: Saint-Nectaire maturation cellars.

The Loire divides cheese-making France in two. Cow's milk cheeses reign in the north, while in the south it is the small savoury goat's cheeses that dominate. However, there is nothing absolute about this division, since the Vosges, Normandy, Brie and Ile-de-France also produce *chèvres* or goat's cheeses, even if relatively few in number and, on the whole, scarcely comparable with the many Pélardons, Picodons and

Crates of Crottins de Chavignol (RIGHT). CENTRE: Chabichou du Poitou. FAR RIGHT: Crottin de Chavignol. OPPOSITE: an assortment of goat's cheeses from the Loire.

Chevrotins of the Cévennes, the Dauphiné, and Provence! The bend of the Loire nonetheless remains a goat's cheese country par excellence, producing as it does innumerable and often truly exquisite specimens, even if they have not achieved the fame of the five local AOCs: Crottin de Chavignol, Selles-sur-Cher, Pouligny-Saint-Pierre, Sainte-Maure, and Chabichou du Poitou. This specialisation so characteristic of the region no doubt arises from the nature of the soil, which is less rich than further north, as well as from the arrival, some two millennia ago, of small livestock raisers who brought, along with their goats and sheep, a taste for the cheeses that today are consumed fresh in the summer or hard-ripened in the winter.

CHABICHOU DU POITOU

This is the latest of the region's AOCs. With its special qualities now officially recognised, the little Poitevin cheese has come to enjoy increased production. *Chabi*, a local term derived from the Arabic *chebli* meaning goat, signifies nothing more than a small goat's cheese. Farmhouse Chabichou is delicious up until autumn, whereas dairy-made is best from spring to summer.

■ CHABICHOU DU POITOU

Goat's milk cheese (45% fat)

TYPE: soft, natural rind

SHAPE: round, slightly conical, 6 cm in diameter at the base, 5 cm at the top, 6 cm thick

WEIGHT: 100 g

MATURATION: about 1 month in a cool, humid cellar

PRESENTATION: as is, on straw

CROTTIN DE CHAVIGNOL

This little cheese from the region of Berry merits its name only when sufficiently ripe and dry, even if lovers of goat's cheese prefer it supple, while the thick rind is still forming. Also much appreciated hot on toasts or in salads.

■ CROTTIN DE CHAVIGNOL

Goat's milk cheese (45% fat)

TYPE: soft, natural rind covered by spots of white, blue, or brown mould

SHAPE: round, 5 cm in diameter, 2 cm thick

WEIGHT: around 60 g

MATURATION: from 15 days to 2 months; for thoroughly hardened cheeses, in a dry, ventilated cellar

PRESENTATION: as is

CENTRAL EUROPE

The crocus is an alpine flower, appearing on the damp meadows as the snow melts, at altitudes of up to 2700 metres (BELOW).

BOTTOM: Gruyère.
CENTRE: Gruyère being pressed in a dairy in the village of Moléson, in the canton of Fribourg.
TOP RIGHT: Schabzieger.
OPPOSITE: a grandiose mountain of Swiss cheeses, featuring Gruyère, Sbrinz, Appenzeller and Emmental among others.

it was not until 1602, when a delegation from the French embassy paid an official visit, that it was actually recorded as Gruyère for the first time. Despite the fact it has smaller holes, is both denser and harder, and its weight rarely exceeds the 35 kg mark, it is often confused with Emmental. Today, it is still made according to traditional methods. Gruyère owes its hardness to the fact that the curds are only heated once they are clotted. As a young cheese, the subtle perfume it emanates is one of alpine flowers. Later, when mature, it takes on the full flavour of a great cheese.

■ GRUYÈRE
Full-fat cow's milk cheese (45% fat)
TYPE: hard, with little round holes and the occasional crack; hard, slightly moist rind
SHAPE: round, 50 cm in diameter
WEIGHT: 20 to 35 kg
MATURATION: 4 to 10 months
PRESENTATION: the rind is marked with "Switzerland" and "Gruyère"

SCHABZIEGER

Schabzieger is very different from other Swiss cheeses which often weigh several dozen kilos. This one is a little truncated cone, somewhat greenish with a very spicy taste, and weighs no more than 200 g. It is said to be a very old monastery cheese from the canton of Glarus, to which cheese-makers of the epoch apparently added meadow fenugreek, a clover brought back from

the East by the Crusaders in the 11th century. This is the plant to which the cheese owes both its distinctive flavour and its international success, especially in the United States where it goes by the name of Sapsago. Schabzieger contains no fat, and this also contributes to its popularity. It is made from skimmed cow's milk to which lactic acid has been added. After this, it is heated to just under 100° C. Once cooled down again, the curds are pressed into a cone shape, then matured in a warm atmosphere (20° C) and dried. Schabzieger is also sold in powdered form as a condiment.

■ SCHABZIEGER
Fully-skimmed cow's milk cheese
TYPE: firm, rindless
SHAPE: little cone (also sold as a powder)
WEIGHT: 100 to 200 g
MATURATION: several months

SBRINZ

This is probably the oldest hard cheese from the central Alps. As far back as Roman times, Sbrinz already had the desired qualities for a cheese: it travelled well and could be carried by the legionnaires on their colonial expeditions as easily as it could be transported to Rome. In the 1st century AD, Pliny was already talking about the "enchanting presence" of a *caseus helveticus*, or Swiss cheese, very similar to the one we know today. Thanks to the present policy of AOC designation, Sbrinz has regained its fame of yesteryear. Its long maturation period renders it perfectly digestible, to such an extent that it is

poured into goatskins for a lengthy maturation which may last up to 12 months.

Posni Sir, another sheep's cheese from Montenegro, has different names according to its place of origin (Tord, Mrsav, etc.)

Cheeses on display at the market in Montenegro (RIGHT). BOTTOM: sheep in the Bulgarian countryside. TOP RIGHT: blue cheeses maturing in a natural cellar, near the village of Mikra in Bulgaria.

Kashkaval, a *pasta filata* cheese found all across eastern Europe, finds its equivalent in Presukaca. This smooth cheese from Bosnia-Herzegovnia, is made by dipping the drained curds into hot water.

Licki is a traditional smoked cheese made by shepherds of the region in years gone by.

Paski is a cow's milk cheese similar in type and texture to Parmesan.

Travnik, a full-fat sheep's cheese probably of Armenian origin, is known well beyond its region of production, Bosnia. Its popularity is due to its mildness and the fullness of its flavour resulting from the goat's milk added to it.

Katschkawalj, one of Bulgaria's great cheeses, is said to have been introduced by soldiers of the Roman Empire. Be this as it may, it was the Slavs and the nomadic Bulgars, ancestors of today's occupants, arriving in the 6th century, who introduced yoghurt and the other great national cheese, Sirene. From the 14th to 19th centuries, Bulgaria lived under Ottoman rule, and this was not without its influence on native eating habits. Sheep's cheeses became common fare even though the mountain regions remained faithful to their beloved hard cheeses. In 1878 Bulgaria won its independence, only to lose it again in 1947 under Soviet influence. While collectivisation of the land and mechanisation of farming-practice favoured development of the cheese-making industry, a generalised exodus from the land could not be avoided. The famous Bulgarian Yoghurt is not, strictly speaking, a cheese, since lactic

ferment is used rather than rennet. People say that if Bulgarians and other people living around the Black Sea and the Caucasus live so long, it is because of the yoghurt. Traditional yoghurt is made by heating the milk until it has reduced by a third. Once cooled, the lactic ferment of *Thermobacterium bulgaricum* and *Streptococcus thermophilus* found in plants are added. Bulgarian peasants and shepherds used to use another method as well: they poured the slightly cooled milk into a receptacle having previously contained yoghurt and the fermentation would start off again, or they would mix some ready-made yoghurt with boiled milk.

KATSCHKAWALJ

This sheep's cheese is very similar to its Romanian counterpart and, consequently, distantly related to the Italian cow's cheese Caciocavallo. In earlier times, every Bulgarian peasant knew how to prepare it but these days it is generally produced in industrial dairies.

After renneting, the curds are cut up and stirred to allow the whey to run off faster. They are then pressed into a container, kneaded into a large ball, and liberally salted with cooking-salt. During its two-months' maturation, the cheese is kept humid by sprinkling salt water over it. While maturing, it also caves in and takes on the shape of a disc with a protuberance in the middle. Starting off straw-yellow, it gradually picks up a somewhat stronger colour as time moves on. A similar cheese to this, BALCAN or BALCANSKI KATSCHKAWALJ, weighing some 10 kg, is made in the Balkan mountains. But DEMI-BALCAN, like all other cheeses made in the lowlands, is softer and slightly smaller.

■ KATSCHKAWALJ

Full-fat sheep's milk cheese (50% fat)

TYPE: pressed, hard; dry rind

SHAPE: round

WEIGHT: 7 to 9 kg

MATURATION: 2 months; it becomes more bitter to the taste as maturation continues

SIRENE

This is the Bulgarian equivalent of the Romanians' Brinza and the Greeks' Feta. Sirene is a real "common or garden" cheese in Bulgaria and elsewhere. Being quite simply the word for cheese, Sirene represents virtually three quarters of the national cheese production. Traditional Sirene is made from full-fat sheep's milk, and the easily broken, semi-hard cheese is kept in tins or barrels filled with brine. Cow's milk Sirene, a much more countrified cheese, is softer than the others.

■ SIRENE

Full-fat sheep's or cow's milk cheese (45% fat)

TYPE semi-hard; without rind

WEIGHT: 7 to 9 kg

MATURATION: preserved in brine

As was their wont with all the countries they conquered, the Romans introduced their own cheese-making techniques into Romania. In all probability, their contacts with the Indo-European race of Dacians, who were big milk drinkers, taught the Romans the art of *pasta filata* cheese-making. Throughout the long years of turmoil in the Middle Ages, populations sought refuge in the Carpathian mountains where ancient cheese-making traditions were still upheld. After Romania lost the rich province of Moldavia at the end of the Second World War, and all the farmland had been collectivised, dairy production was mainly intended for export. Imitations of foreign cheeses were preferred to the detriment of traditional products. And although the

Romanian wooden cheese moulds from the beginning of the century (ABOVE). TOP: Sirene. BOTTOM LEFT: Katschkawalj. BOTTOM RIGHT: Romanian cheese-makers draining the curds in front of their wooden hut out in the meadows.

latter might have been few and far between, they did provide the local populations with vital food.

BRINZA

Brinza, whose name means cheese in the Carpathian region, was the traditional cheese of sheep-farmers in central Europe and the Near East. This mild, almost soft cheese is still family-fare today. The curds are broken up, pressed, then cut into bits. It is eaten fresh but may also be preserved over the winter in salted milk.

BURDUF BRINZA, or cheese in a bag, is matured in sheep- or goatskin bags using salted whey. Depending on the size of the skin, the cheese can weigh from 15 to 50 kg.

COCHULETZ BRINZA starts off as salted and kneaded Brinza which is then matured in the bark of fir trees to enhance its flavour.

A low-fat, soft cheese flavoured with herbs, URDA, is made from the whey of Brinza.

■ BRINZA

Ful -fat sheep's milk cheese (45% fat)

TYPE: soft; without rind

WEIGHT: 3 to 60 kg

MATURATION: preserved in salted milk in metal containers

Brinza (TOP).
BOTTOM: Halloumi in tresses.

HALLOUMI

A traditional cheese made along similar lines to *pasta filata* cheeses, Halloumi is much copied abroad where it is sold in various forms. Romanian Halloumi is worked into tresses about 20 cm long, and sold in tubs of low-salt brine where it completes its maturation.

■ HALLOUMI

Cow's milk cheese (45% fat)

TYPE: pressed, firm, sometimes with holes, slightly elastic, white to pale yellow; rindless

SHAPE: 20 cm-long tresses

MATURATION: preserved in iron tubs

The Czechs and Slovaks, despite a common language and origin, have distinctly separate histories; linked to Germany and Austria for the former, and Hungary the latter. Bohemia-Moravia geared itself towards the industrial world of the west, whereas Slovakia – an essentially farming land – has long kept its eyes turned towards the east. The cheeses reflect this dichotomy with strong, hard goat's cheeses in the Czech territories (just like certain border zones between Germany and Austria), and Brinza type sheep's cheeses in Slovakia. In such a mountainous terrain, small-scale farming is a natural choice, and so is making cheeses, and these, far from being pale imitations of the originals, leave a taste in the mouth that reminds one of the rugged landscapes of old central Europe. Today, goat's and sheep's milk is sometimes replaced by cow's, or by a mixture. Industrial cheeses similar to Gouda or Emmental may also be found.

ABERTAM

The mountainous north-west of Bohemia is an area where Germany's influence can be felt even in the cheeses. Abertam is a hard sheep's

milk cheese with a rather strong flavour. It is made in Karlovy-Vary, a spa resort known previously as Carslbad. Crowned heads and great artists of the 19th century – Johannes Brahms, Frédéric Chopin and Alexander Pushkin – used to come here to give their stomachs a cure. Who knows, maybe some of the town's big hotels used to keep Abertam on the menu...

■ ABERTAM

Full-fat sheep's milk cheese (45% fat)

Type: pressed, hard, thin rind

Shape: ball

Weight: 500 g

Maturation: 2 months

OSCHTJEPKA

This is a very old sheep's cheese that shepherds living in the Carpathian mountains used to make. Its smooth plasticity is fairly reminiscent of Kashkaval. Made from sour milk, it is moulded into the shape of a large orange, then matured for a few days in brine. After this, it is smoked over a wood fire in the traditional manner. PARENICA is a Slovakian cheese similar to Oschtjepka in shape and consistency. This too, used to be and still is made by shepherds.

■ OSCHTJEPKA

Sheep's or cow's milk cheese, sometimes mixed (less than 45% fat)

Type: pressed, semi-hard; with thin, dark-coloured rind

Shape: round

Weight: 500 g

Maturation: 1 week, then smoked

OTHER CHEESES

BRYNDZA, like Hungarian Liptauer, is a cheese produced on the Slovakian side of the Carpathian mountains, and is also made in two separate stages. The shepherds prepare lumps, weighing several kilos, from sheep's milk curds which they then drain in a cloth hanging from the rafters. The cheese is salted and matured for about a week, then sold to the nearest dairy which breaks them up to make the Bryndza.

The fertile basins found in Moravia are ideal for stock-breeding. This is where they make OLMÜTZER QUARGEL, a cheese derived from sour sheep's and cow's milk that does not differ greatly from Austria's Quark. The salted curds are kneaded into an older soft white cheese, then matured in a barrel or iron container for 2 months. In the north of Bohemia, RIESENGEBIRGE, a soft cheese bearing the same name as the mountain chain from which it comes, is manufactured from goat's milk and matured in humid cellars for a few days. The same region also produces KOPPEN, a large and very perfumed goat's cheese with a fairly strong smell, weighing about one kilo.

Abertam (TOP LEFT). CENTRE: Oschtjepka. BELOW: a brightly painted house in Prague's "Street of Gold".

Poland is a vast plain stretching out to the north, east and west and hemmed in only by the Carpathian massif in the south. Since time immemorial, it has attracted the covetous eyes of its German, Russian and Swedish neighbours. And with a history as chaotic as Poland's it is not surprising her people have not been able to develop many original cheeses of their own, despite the huge land area allowing them to graze large numbers of animals.

The country began to form in the 10th century through the union of Slavic tribes from the Oder and Vistula basins. Kraków and Warsaw became major economic and cultural centres, trading with other commercial towns of the League who dealt in hard Dutch cheeses. In those days, Poland produced cheeses similar to these and sold them far beyond its borders. The Second World War brought in its wake massive destruction of Poland's towns, country and cities and local cheeses were unable to survive the turmoil.

Among the few remaining traditional cheeses still made is TYLZSCKI, resembling Tilsit from which it takes its name. This is the only local product which does not come from the

mountains in the south. Nowadays, it is made in dairies, as is TRAPISTAW, a soft, washed-rind Trappist cheese. As to PODHALANSKI, this is a semi-hard cow's or sheep's milk cheese with little holes and a firm rind. It is sold in loaf-like slabs, sometimes smoked in the way it used to be when peasants stored their cheeses by the fireside. TWAROGOWY and OLSZTYNSKI are both traditional cheeses from the mountainous regions in the south; they are still made in the old-fashioned way from skimmed milk. The former is prepared from cow's or sheep's milk, the latter is a variety of this which undergoes maturation in a barrel of brine. Today, Poland manufactures a range of industrial cheeses in the style of Gouda, Edam, Camembert, Cheddar and Emmental.

Throughout the entire Baltic region, the cheeses are all of the Tilsit type. Once German, the town of Tilsit was annexed at the end of the Second World War by the USSR and renamed Sovietsk. And so, the Sovietskis found in all the towns of the former Soviet Union are in fact Tilsits. They are manufactured in industrial cheese plants, far from their original starting-points. The variety found in Latvia is called LATVIISKI. It is a very salty cow's milk cheese in the shape of a slab, weighing from 2 to 2.5 kg, and matured in a humid atmosphere.

■ SOVIETSKI

Cow's milk cheese (50% fat)

TYPE: pressed, hard; slightly moist rind

SHAPE: slab

WEIGHT: from 10 to 15 kg

MATURATION: at least 2 months

Podhalanski (ABOVE).
TOP: the gloriously decorated interior of a farm in Zalipia, in Little Poland (Malopolska), situated on the upper plateaux of the Odra and the Vistula, overlooked by the Holy Cross massif.
BOTTOM RIGHT: a typical Lithuanian farmhouse.

The Slavs probably learned about cheese and cheese-making during the 1st millennium from the Greeks with whom they had numerous contacts. Similarly, very early on, the Slavs learnt how to prepare a delicious soft white cheese, and it is equally possible they perfected a cheese-making technology, albeit archaic. Records from the past inform us that as far back as the 10th century they were consuming an enormous amount of milk to make not only sweet desserts, but also soft and fermented cheeses. On the other hand, the peoples from the north and east – especially those who lived, and still live, above the Arctic Circle – consume but very few dairy products of any sort, including cheese.

During a journey to Holland, Peter the First of Russia took the opportunity to

try some of the local cheeses. He liked them. To benefit from their know-how, he invited several famous master cheese-makers to Russia. It was not until 1795 however, that the first cheese plant was built on Russian soil, and not until 1860 that Russia's first cheese-maker, Verchiagin, could distinguish himself. He decided to take a serious look at agriculture and went off to study

dairy production in Switzerland. On his return, he set about providing the cheese-makers of his own country with training, and also organised an immense educational campaign on cheese, publishing bulletins, articles, etc. Subsequent collectivisation of land resulted in uniform products. It is a great shame that no census on cheese was carried out at the turn of the century. Nevertheless, a number of typical cheeses produced on the *kolkhozes*, or cooperative State farms, are worth mentioning. MOSKOVSKI is one of them; it is an elastic, pressed cheese weighing

5 to 8 kg, though full of big holes visible when it is cut open. Another is CHLETSARSKI, a round cheese weighing 50 to 100 kg which, after maturing for at least six months, can be kept for a year, if not two. STEPNOI and KOSTROMSKOI are hard, rectangular cheeses of the Gouda type, both weighing about 5 or 6 kg. In preparing processed cheese, the Russians prefer to use those that are already unctuous, such as Sovietski (or Tilsit). They are packaged in rectangular slabs of about 100 g, or in 50-g squares. Sometimes, they may even be wrapped in gut (which explains why they look like sausages) or greaseproof paper, before smoke-curing them.

Russian alphabet primer illustrated with various country activities to help teach the language (BOTTOM LEFT). CENTRE: a view of the Russian agricultural landscape.
TOP: Sovietski.
ABOVE: a birch-bark box showing sheep-shearing and weaving scenes. BELOW: cheese-makers from the Ukraine wearing traditional costume.

If the Bulgarians say they live so long because of their yoghurt, the Caucasians put their longevity down to KEFIR. This centuries-old foodstuff was created by peoples of Indo-European origin, large numbers of whom live in this region. It is the recommended drink for all those suffering from digestive disorders. Kefir can be found almost everywhere in eastern Europe and even in Germany, but it has never claimed to be a cheese. It is in fact simply fermented milk. Whether it comes from sheep, cows, or even camels, the milk is fermented by adding a yeast, called kefir seeds. One of the best-known specialities found in the cheese-making country of Armenia is a cow's or sheep's milk cheese called TCHANAKH. It is preserved in brine and stored in vats.

EREVAN sheep's or cow's milk cheese, or EREVANSKI, is a semi-hard cheese kept in brine-filled containers or barrels.

A pagan temple in Armenia, from the 1st century AD (BELOW). TOP: a goatherd and his goats. Painting by Piros Manishivilli Niko (early 20th century). *Georgia State Museum, Tbilissi.*

Unlike other Armenian cheeses, SOULOUGOUNI does find its way outside its local region. This is another cheese which is preserved in brine.

TELPANIR uses the skimmed, sour milk of cows or sheep, and is matured in wooden boxes for about a week. This name is of Turkish origin (*peynir* meaning cheese in Turkish), but it can also be known as LEAF, ZWIRN or TSCHIL. In the Caucasus and Georgia, it is quite traditional to keep cheeses in brine. This is the case for MOTAL and KOBIISKI, both made from either cow's or sheep's milk. BRYNZA, fairly similar to its Romanian homonym, is manufactured from cow's or sheep's milk in these regions too. Although, as a language, Ossetic is rarely spoken except by a few very old people in front of the microphones of linguists come to record these living

"libraries", its cheese, OSSETIN, remains much-appreciated fare. Once the sheep's or cow's milk is renneted, the fragmented curds are then put to boil. When they have become nice and compact, they are kneaded with whey and moulded into round cheeses. Lastly, having been salted, they are matured in brine for several months.

East of the Caucasus, beyond the Caspian Sea to the edges of the Altay chain, and right up to the boundaries of Turkestan and China, hard and semi-hard, pressed cow's milk cheeses such as the 20 kg millstone-shaped ALTAISKI can be found. It is more than likely however, that they are imported cheeses. The genuine Altay cheese would seem to be GORNYALTAJSKI. This is made from full-fat sheep's cheese. The orange mould that forms on the rind is prevented from proliferating by brushing it regularly. There is another variety, a smoked one, which can be kept for a very long while and, just like Parmesan, is eaten when very hard. *Gorny,* meaning "mountain", is the generic term for cheeses from the mountainous regions of the southern former Soviet Union. DARALAGJAZSKY, which is made in cooperatives, is fairly widespread and well-known. The milk used may be cow's or sheep's or both, and, once the curds are salted, garlic and thyme are added. Maturation takes place in a sheepskin bag.

■ DARALAGJAZSKY

Cow's or sheep's milk cheese

(at least 25% fat)

TYPE: soft, white, sometimes flavoured

with herbs

SHAPE: according to container

WEIGHT: 10 to 15 kg

MATURATION: in a sheepskin bag

or a bottle

VOLJSKI is a product from the Volga Basin. It is a cow's cheese with a elastic texture and thin rind which is sold in slabs of 2 to 3 kg. PIKHANTNYJ is a fuller-flavoured, spicy version of it. VOLOGODSKI, coming from the same region, is a circular, smoked cheese weighing 2 kg.

DESSERTNYJ BELYJ is an industrially-manufactured, soft, cow's milk cheese requiring 1 week for maturation. Another variety of this, Dessertnyj, is sprinkled with *Penicillium candidum* during its 10-day maturation, and this provides it with a bloomy rind. ZAKUSSOTCHNY is a soft cow's milk cheese that takes a month to mature and, for some strange reason, is sometimes called Camembert; it bears no resemblance whatsoever. LIOUBITELSKI, the "lovers' cheese"

is a recent creation and can be found literally everywhere. It is an industrially-produced cheese that "resembles" Camembert too, but only if you have never seen one.

Originally from the Carpathians, KARPATSKI, just like KUBANSKI (from the Kuban) is one of the firm or hard mountain cheeses with or without holes made in the Ukraine.

Goats in front of the picturesque window of a farm in Siberia (LEFT). FAR LEFT: Daralagjazsky. BOTTOM: a herd of cattle fording a river in the Volga Basin.

LANDS OF THE SUN

The prophet Mohammed it may be remembered, viewed milk with suspicion, symbol as it was of the nomadic life of the Arabs he longed to unify in the new Islamic faith. A famous *hadj* quoted him as saying: "What I fear for my people is milk, with the devil hiding in it between the froth and the cream. Those Moslems who drink it] will go back to the desert, abandoning the centre where people pray together".

Nonetheless, cheese has been made around the Mediterranean for thirty centuries. And it was the shepherd's concert that gave birth to pastoral poetry, such as the *Idylls* of Theocritus. These songs tell that when he fell in love with the naiad Galatea, the roguish Polyphemus, the Cyclops of the *Odyssey,* sacrificed his shepherdess, who was guilty of loving the disturbing Acis. So-called bucolic customs should often be taken with a pinch of salt. In his *Bucolics,* Virgil does no more than mention, among other traditions, those of souring and curdling, which still form the basis of Mediterranean cuisine. The Muses were the daughters of "memory" and shepherds did have their pastimes. This pastoral idyll, so closely linked to the history of cheese, was still flourishing in Poussin's classicism: "Et in Arcadia ego!" All the oldest cheeses are made from sheep's or goat's milk: clearly a telling fact. Personally, I am always careful not to miss those summers in Provence when, as the poet Pierre-Emmanuel puts it: "The Gods come to visit the blue and transparent hills". According bees the spiritual quality they used to be attributed in Antiquity, one could say that cheeses from sunny climes are, as it were, lived in and "pollenated" by these social insects. Such seemingly outdated techniques as curdling – a homely, almost "ecological" custom – take me back to memories of my childhood in the Ardèche. These traditions have been kept alive in the Larzac, in inland Corsica, in southern Italy, in Greece, and far away on the Turkish shores·of Byzantium and in the distant mountains of Anatolia. They are part of a set of practices and a way of life a very far cry from our own customs, so driven and dessicated by Malthusian violence. The poets have always known this, condemning the putrescence of our cities.

I think of my own corner of the Mediterranean in the first flush of summer: the foothills of the Pre-Alps, with the Contadour and Giono's beloved hills, which come to life amid all the sweet-chestnut flowers, the far-off slopes of the Aigoual and the Causses. A certain famous sheep's cheese is made in this area, in Roquefort-sur-Soulzon. Here, the limestone peak of the Cambalou harbours many natural rock galleries used by the cheese-makers to mature their produce. During its stay there, it is fanned by a

Lebney, a cheese found in almost all Middle Eastern countries, is often preserved in jars of herb-flavoured olive oil. PRECEDING PAGES: goats in a farmyard in Cyprus.

196

A Cretan cheese-seller put into the shade by his wares.

flow of soft damp air, laden with spores made fertile by these natural cellars. This mysterious process would be worthless without the special character of sheep's milk from the Causses – complemented by those of Corsica or the Pyrenees – which form the right kind of curds, admirably suited to such a maturation in natural cellars. The story continues on the other side of the Pyrenees and their criss-crossing shepherds' tracks, with the civilisation of old Castile: Góngora, Lope de Vega and Cervantes all celebrated bucolic customs. The great pilgrimage route for cheese starts in far-off Asia Minor, passing through Greece, Campania, and Narbonne. It follows the sun's path across the Mediterranean. So the race of Helios too has its associations with cheese.

An archeology of culinary practices as mirrored by the myths: this is more or less what we seek in these sun-drenched lands. Immemorial, unchanged since the faithful Eumaeus, since the wink which Ulysses sends us across the millenia, from Calypso's cave to the return to Ithaca. Nothing has really changed since the alternate rhymes of Theocritus' shepherds. Corsica, they say, was herself discovered by a shepherdess. This "Island of Beauty" is still nourished on milk. Broccio (or Brucciu) is without doubt an invention of the gods. Under the blackened mantelpiece of her smoking chimney, the mythical shepherdess made curds in a copper cauldron. She used the previous day's cloudy-looking whey, adding pure milk to it while heating the mixture. The "snowflower" would then rise up to the top of the cauldron, a foaminess that she collected in the skimmer, placing the Broccio in a rush mould to give it its shape.

Gorgonzola and Parmesan come from the Lombardy Alps and Emilia. They are made from cow's milk. On the shores of Byzantine Ravenna, the image of the shepherd, the Good Shepherd, surrounded by his sheep, has glittered on down the centuries. Don Quixote spent time with the shepherds on the dried-out earth of Castile, because he wanted to bring back the "Golden Age". And, as all light comes from the East, it is also fitting to evoke the image of Moreh's Oak, where Abraham gathered together three mysterious travellers and offered them cakes of flour, meat and curdled milk. This scene too is depicted in the mosaics of Ravenna, as well as in the shimmering icons of Byzantium: an everyday practice of material civilisation picked out by the highest forms of art. A little sheep's or goat's cheese reminds us of this ancient tradition, and goes well with several bottles of *côtes*, from Côte-de-Nuit to Côte-Rôtie. The marvel of Roquefort is to the biblical curds of Abraham what the triumphal rose window of Chartres, all veined with light, is to the humble eglantine rose. A moving way to sing like Saint Francis, the "Song of Creation" from this plateau of the Causses.

Gorgonzola, the great Italian blue cheese, here shown at a perfect stage of ripeness.

Several well-known Italian cheeses go back to antiquity. Indeed the Romans made widespread use of dairy products. As a concentrated source of food energy, cheese formed part of the diet of the legionnaires campaigning on behalf of the Caesars. Their cheeses had to be hard enough to stand up to the long journeys, the jolting of the bumpy roads, the changes in temperature and the ups and downs of the combat itself. The role played by the ancestors of Parmesan, and all *grana* type cheeses, in the construction and upkeep of the Roman Empire was far from negligeable. Various small buildings used for making and storing cheeses have been discovered in the ruins of Pompeii, and the place of cheese in Roman civilisation is further confirmed in the writings of numerous Latin authors. The richest and most detailed sources of information are the works of Marcus Apicius (25 BC), a famous gastronomist credited with a book of recipes, and Columella (1st century AD), who wrote a treatise on agriculture These days, cheese is made practically everywhere in Italy. Hard sheep's cheeses, which keep for a very long time and mature in a dry environment, are the chief produce of Sicily and the central and southern regions of Italy, as they are of most hot and sunny lands. In the north of the country, cheese-making has been stimulated by the growth of commercial centres and large local markets. Lombardy combines a seaboard, propitious for international trade, with a mountainous hinter and in the form of the Alps and their rich south-facing pastures. Many cheeses from this region are therefore a product of transhumance and the resultant need to use the large quantities of milk yielded by all the various herds before they go up to the mountain pastures (Gorgonzola, Taleggio, etc). The fertile plain of Emilia-Romagna was the birthplace of the famous Parmesan (Parmigiano-Reggiano) itself, which is a cow's cheese as hard as certain sheep's cheeses, normally used in grated form. Italian cheeses spread across the world at the same rate as the Italians themselves, pasta and pizzas being the best ambassadors of Parmesan, Provolone and Mozzarella.

ASIAGO

This pasteurised cow's milk cheese, produced in the Veneto, used to be made in the village of Asiago (Vicenza province) from sheep's milk.

It spawned several different varieties. ASIAGO PRESSATO is a full fat semi-cooked pressed cheese, made from unskimmed milk, with a 45% fat content. Its rind is thin and elastic. The holes in this cheese are slightly larger than for Asiago made with skimmed milk. Asiago Pressato can be consumed after 1 month of maturation. It is sold in rounds 30 to 40 cm in diameter and 11 to 15 cm deep for a weight varying from 11 to 15 kg. ASIAGO D'ALLEVO is made either from the milk from two milkings, one of which is skimmed, or from one milking partially skimmed. It is either salted dry, or by immersion in brine. When it has matured for more than a year it is used as a grating cheese.

■ ASIAGO

Cow's milk cheese (34% fat)

TYPE: pressed, semi-hard uncooked cheese, granular for old Asiago; smooth rind

A milkmaid in the costume of the Liguria region, 1820 (ABOVE).

BELOW: Venice in the 15th century; painting by Gentile Bellini. *Accademia Gallery, Venice.*

OPPOSITE: a Parmesan being carried through the streets of Siena.

SHAPE: round, straight-sided

weight: 8 to 12 kg

MATURATION: 1, 2 or 6 months for dessert cheese; 1 year for grating cheese.

CACIOCAVALLO

This is the oldest existing *pasta filata* cheese. Its origins are lost in the mists of time. It was mentioned as early as the 1st century in the famous treatise of the Roman writer, Columella, but it seems that its beginnings go back even beyond the Romans, who included it in their menus. Tradition has it that its name derives from "horseback cheese", and that horsemen at one time suspended it from either side of their saddles in pouches made of leather or cloth, strung together by a rope. Caciocavallo is reminiscent of cheeses from the Caucasus and Central Asia, which are matured in sheep's skin or goatskin bags. It may originally have been made from mare's milk. Does it follow perhaps that the ancestors of Caciocavallo once fed Attila's horsemen and the peoples of the great invasions? The slightly elastic consistency of this *pasta filata* cheese is obtained by a process similar to that which has made the fortune of Mozzarella cheese.

The curd is placed in whey and heated to 45° C, then it is cut into thin strips and plunged into hot water and whey again. Next it is hand-kneaded, then put once more into hot water. After it has been shaped, it is cooled by immersion in water, this last being the only part of the process that differs from Mozzarella production. The cheese is usually shaped into the form of a gourd

or pear, and a hemp loop fastened around the pointed end, so that the cheese can be hung up to mature, for a period of 3 months under dry conditions, during which time it is cleaned and oiled regularly. This maturation process may sometimes be prolonged for a further 3 months. Caciocavallo is an AOC cheese. Its flavour is mild and delicate when lightly matured, but left longer it becomes increasingly strong, and is then used as a grating cheese. This southern European cheese has an extended family. Numerous *pasta filata* cheeses called CACIOTTE are produced in Tuscany, Umbria, and the regions around Urbino and Rome. Central European Kashkaval cheeses are also distant relations or this large tribe, not including Provolone, which is a direct descendant of Caciocavallo.

■ CACIOCAVALLO

Cow's milk cheese (44% fat)

TYPE: pressed, *filata*, often smoked; thin,

Shepherds and sheep, from a fresco by Gozzoli Benozo. *Palazzo Riccardi, Florence* (ABOVE). TOP RIGHT: Caciocavallo. RIGHT: the livestock market in Rome (anonymous work).

smooth, oiled, golden yellow or light
brown rind

SHAPE: large pear shape with a smaller
swelling at the top

Weight: 3 to 4 kg

MATURATION: 3 to 6 months

CRESCENZA

This full fat soft cheese, made in
Lombardy, is a *stracchino*, so-called
after *stracche,* which means soft or
tired in Lombardy dialect. Although
it is not a mouldy cheese, Crescenza is
closely related to Gorgonzola, but as it
is not made in the same place it has no
right to the latter's prestigious name. It
is also fresher and looser-textured than
Gorgonzola. It matures very quickly,
taking only a week in cool conditions.

■ CRESCENZA

Cow's milk cheese (48% fat)

TYPE: soft, white to pale yellow
coloured; rindless

SHAPE: slab, 18 by 4 cm

MATURATION: 8 to 10 days

PRESENTATION: greaseproof paper backed
with silver paper marked with
the brand name.

FIORE SARDO

Fiore Sardo ("Flower of Sardinia")
is also known as PECORINO SARDO
or Sardinian sheep's cheese. Like all
sheep's milk cheeses, it can be eaten
either fresh or matured. Accordingly,
shepherds used to eat the cheese
fresh in their daily diet but also to keep
some maturing to sell later at market.
In the 16th century, Sardinian cheeses
were more widely-sold than any other
over the entire Mediterranean area.

■ FIORE SARDO

Sheep's milk cheese (minimum 40% fat)

TYPE: soft or very mature and hard, from
white to straw coloured depending
on maturity; hard hazelnut coloured rind

SHAPE: squat barrel

WEIGHT: 1 to 4 kg

MATURATION: up to 6 months

FONTINA

This cheese is usually used for
fondues, but it is delicious when eaten
from the block, especially if it is
summer Fontina, made with the milk
of cows grazing on a pine meadows at
an altitude of 2000 m, where the lush
grass is composed of species unique to
these pastures. Fontina is a speciality
of the mountainous Val d'Aoste region,
overlooked by Mont Blanc.
FONTAL, an imitation of Fontina,
is a second class cheese, since its
production area is poorly defined, falling
partly in France and partly in Italy.
It is often used for raclettes and for
preparing certain other dishes. A round
of Fontal measures from 40 to 45 cm
in diameter and is 8 to 10 cm thick.
It weighs between 10 and 16 kilos.

Crescenza (FAR
LEFT). CENTRE: milking
sheep in Italy.
TOP: Fiore Sardo.

■ FONTINA

Cow's milk cheese (45% fat)

TYPE: pressed, cooked, with a few small

holes; brushed and sometimes oiled

rind, light brown coloured

SHAPE: large round, 45 cm in diameter,

8 to 10 cm thick

WEIGHT: 8 to 18 kg

MATURATION: 3 months

Fontina (TOP).

BELOW: the Gorgonzola

factory in Novara

at the beginning

of the 20th century.

FAR RIGHT: Gorgonzola.

GORGONZOLA

This is one of the world's great cheeses. It comes from a small town, lying north of Milan in Lombardy, and takes its name from this town, where it was first made more than 1000 years ago. Since time immemorial, the cattle herds have stopped off at Gorgonzola on their way back from the mountains, before separating out to return to their respective villages for the winter.
The milk is coagulated using calves' rennet, at 28 to 32° C. The curds are laid in layers in a mould lined with fine canvas. The bottom, the sides and the top are coated with the hot curds from the morning's milking. The cold curds of the evening's milking are then poured into the middle. The cheeses are taken out of the moulds but kept in the canvas, and left upside-down to drain for 24 hours. The canvas is then removed and they are put back into the moulds, salted and turned over several times during the following week.
After a first maturation, which takes less than 2 months, holes are made in the cheese to allow the *Penicillium* to penetrate. The second phase of maturation lasts another few weeks. These days, Gorgonzola is matured using an industrial process.
DOLCELATTE, or "sweet milk", is a recent imitation of Gorgonzola, produced in the Pavia region of Lombardy, using pasteurised cow's milk. It is seeded with *Penicillium* after 45 days of maturation, and shaped into the form of a half-log 28 centimetres in diameter and 8 cm deep.
PANARONE is a rapidly matured Gorgonzola, to which no *Penicillium* is added, so it is not a blue marbled cheese. There is also a cheese sold simply under the name of STRACCHINO, which used to be made from the milk of cows on their way back from the mountains. It is a full fat soft, rindless cheese, containing 48% fat. It is sold in square blocks 25 by 25 cm and 4 to 5 cm thick, weighing 1 to 4 kg.
GORGONZOLA "CON MASCARPONE" likewise merits a mention.

■ GORGONZOLA

Cow's milk cheese (minimum 48% fat)

TYPE: soft, green veined; natural grey rind,

with brand name stamped on in red

SHAPE: cylindrical, 25 to 30 cm

in diameter, 16 to 20 cm tall

WEIGHT: 6 to 12 kg

MATURATION: about 2 months

PRESENTATION: in silver paper marked

with brand name

GRANA PADANO

As its name implies, Grana Padano is
a granular cheese native to the Padana
Valley (on the plain of the Po). This AOC
variety of grating cheese has proved
so popular that nowadays it is produced
in every northern Italian province.
It is made in much the same way
as Parmesan. The sole difference lies
in the use of milk from several different
places, which is not at all the case for
Parmesan. Grana Padano is a hard
cheese made from partially skimmed
cow's milk from either the morning
or the evening milking. It is matured for
1 or 2 years at a temperature of 15 to
22° C. The cheese is round-shaped
and can weigh up to 40 kg.

■ GRANA PADANO

　Cow's milk cheese (32% fat)

　TYPE: finely granular, with radial cracks,

　very small holes; oiled, thick rind,

　golden yellow, becoming darker

　SHAPE: large round, 35 to 45 cm

in diameter, 18 to 25 cm thick

WEIGHT: 24 to 40 kg

MATURATION: 1 to 2 years, in a ventilated

space at a temperature of 15 to 22° C

MONTASIO

Like Asiago d'Avello, Montasio is
a cooked and pressed cheese, made
using partially-skimmed cow's milk,
containing 32% fat. Its name is that
of a mountain in Friuli, a former
province of the Veneto. When it has
matured for more than 6 months
Montasio is used as a grating cheese.

■ MONTASIO

　Cow's milk cheese (32% fat)

　TYPE: flexible, dense, with small holes;

　smooth golden yellow to dark

　yellow rind

　SHAPE: large round, 34 to 40 cm

　in diameter and 6 to 10 cm thick

WEIGHT: 5 to 9 kg

MATURATION: 2 to 5 months;

6 to 12 months for grating cheese

MOZZARELLA

Mozzarella cheese is as famous
as Parmesan and has conquered the
world in a similar manner. This success
has been largely due to the
internationalisation of the pizza, in which
it is a star ingredient. The strangest thing
about Mozzarella – at least that produced
in the provinces of Lazio and Campania –

Fruits of the earth,
including a wedge
of cheese that bears
a distinct resemblance
to Grana Padano (TOP).
17th-century painting,
Pitti Palace, Florence.
BOTTOM LEFT: Grana
Padano.
LEFT: Montasio.

Mozzarella (CENTRE).
TOP RIGHT: moulds for
Parmesan. BOTTOM
RIGHT: "Parmigiano
Reggiano". Promotional
postcard (1839).
OPPOSITE: mouth-
watering arrangement
of Italian cheeses,
including Mozzarella
di Bufala, Mozzarella
Affumicata, Parmesan,
Pecorino Romano,
Gorgonzola, Ricotta,
Caciocavallo, and pig-
shaped Scarmorze,
another *pasta filata*
cheese.

is that it is made from buffalo's milk. The buffalo was introduced into Italy as a beast of burden after the 16th century to work on the flood-free land of the northern river valleys, which was mostly turned over to rice cultivation.

Elsewhere in Italy, Mozzarella is in fact prepared from cow's milk. The lumps of cow's milk *fiore di latte* (milk flowers) are smaller in the north (200 g) than in the south (300 g).

The production method for Mozzarella is the same as for all *pasta filata* cheeses. Heated whey is first treated with rennet, and then added to the curds. The whole is left to settle, then the whey is strained off. The curds are then plunged into another bath of heated whey and left there for 30 minutes at a temperature of 45° C. The substance now begins to acquire an elastic consistency. It is cut into strips which are again placed in hot water and whey. The cheese-maker can then set to work on what has become a pliable dough, kneading and stretching it. It is this technique of cutting *(mozzare)* and stretching *(filare)* the cheese which led to the names of Mozzarella and *pasta filata* being given to it back in the 15th century.

The last stage in the process consists of moulding the cheese into large rounded lumps and plunging it one last time into hot whey. It then attains its full elasticity and can be made into all sorts of imaginative shapes: plaits, little sausages, fruits, animals and even small human figures.

MOZZARELLA DI BUFALA is an AOC cheese. MOZZARELLA DI BUFALA AFFUMICATA is smoked over wheat straw, leaves and wood.

■ MOZZARELLA

Soft white cheese made with buffalo's milk (50% fat), or cow's milk (45% fat)

TYPE: *pasta filata*, cooked, elastic, white; rindless

SHAPE: balls, bread-rolls, or various modelled figures

WEIGHT: 100 g to 1 kg

PRESENTATION: kept in salted water or whey

PARMESAN

Known the world over, PARMIGIANO REGGIANO has been branded the king of cheeses by the Italians. These days, no self-respecting plate of spaghetti would dare show its face at table unaccompanied by grated Parmesan. The origins of the cheese are dubious and form the subject of a lively controversy, with the strongest claims for its birthplace being made for 11th century Tuscany and the Parma region in the 13th century. Beyond dispute is the fact that the true Parmesan, made in the area around Parma, Bologna and Mantua, has been entitled to an AOC since 1954. Parmesan is a low fat, pressed, cooked and slowly matured cheese. The cows whose milk is used to make it are fed on a diet consisting largely of lucerne and other rich fodder. The fat content of the cheese is kept down to 32% by the use of a mixture of skimmed milk from the evening's and the morning's milking. It takes

Quality control in the Parmesan cellars in Parma (TOP). BOTTOM: Parmesan. FAR RIGHT: Pecorino Romano.

16 litres of milk to make 1 kg of Parmesan. The Parmesan is matured until the end of the summer of the year following that in which it was made. It is straw coloured with a finely granular texture, and a very delicate taste. Its natural rind, the colour of old gold, is marked all over with the label of origin picked out in dots.

■ PARMESAN

Cow's milk cheese (32% fat)

TYPE: pressed, hard, granular, sprinkled with almost invisible holes, cracks converging in the centre; brushed and oiled rind, old gold

SHAPE: cylinder, 35 to 45 cm in diameter, 18 to 24 cm tall

WEIGHT: about 24 to 35 kg

MATURATION: natural, until the end of the summer of the year following that in which the cheese was made; at least 3 years for the driest (some as long as 10 years)

PECORINO ROMANO

Romulus and Remus may have been nurtured on wolf's milk but their contemporaries had long been drinking the milk of goats and sheep. Pecorino Romano is the sheep's cheese produced in the Lazio region, the countryside around Rome. *Pecora* means ewe in Italian; hence the generic term *pecorino* for Italian sheep's cheeses in general, and in particular those which are hard and cooked. Pecorino Romano is made from November to June. Unskimmed sheep's milk is heated, then made into curds using lamb's rennet. The drying takes at least a month and the maturation goes on for 8 months under dry conditions. The rind is coated in oil during the maturation. Yellow clay or tallow used to be added at the end of the maturation period. Pecorino Romano may be eaten grated or straight from the block.

PECORINO SICILIANO is a hard, cooked sheep's cheese containing grains of pepper. It is matured for 4 months and weighs approximately 12 kg.

■ PECORINO ROMANO

Sheep's milk cheese (36% fat)

TYPE: pressed, cooked or uncooked, semi-hard, granular, straw coloured; smooth rind, coated in tallow or olive oil

SHAPE: cylindrical, 20 to 25 cm in diameter, 14 to 22 cm tall

WEIGHT: 8 to 22 kg

MATURATION: 1 month (drying time), then 8 months.

PROVOLONE

The most famous descendent of Caciocavallo, similarly made using unskimmed cow's milk and the same method. The mild variety is obtained by using calves' rennet, while the stronger form is made with kid goats' rennet. In the north of the country, where a substantial milk yield is guaranteed by the mountains and rich pastures, Provolone is often made to a larger size than in the rest of Italy. It can be shaped like a pear, a cone or a thick sausage. The biggest cheeses sometimes used to weigh as much as several dozen kilos.

Among the other *pasta filata* cheeses, INCANESTRATO merits a mention here. It is a Sicilian *pasta filata* cheese made with sheep's or cow's milk, and sometimes seasoned with pepper. PROVATURA is made from buffalo's milk, as is PROVOLE. Both should be eaten fresh.

Another cow's milk *pasta filata* cheese is produced in the area surrounding Ragusa in Sicily and called RAGUSANO. It is sold in squarish slabs weighing 6 to 12 kg. Like certain other *pasta filata* cheeses, Ragusano is strung up to mature in pairs. When it has matured for more than 6 months, it is used as a grating cheese.

■ PROVOLONE

Cow's milk cheese (44% fat)

TYPE: pressed *pasta filata*, very dense; smooth, thin, golden to brownish yellow rind

SHAPE: hand-moulded into truncated cones, pears, etc.

WEIGHT: 1 to 6 kg

MATURATION: 2 to 3 months

RICOTTA

Italy produces a large number of soft white cheeses, including Ricotta, Fiore Sardo and CAPRINO, which is made with goat's milk, as its name suggests. Ricotta goes back at least to classical times and perhaps as far as the original introduction of sheep and goats into the western Mediterranean. It is not really a cheese in the strict sense of the term but it has made its name as one. It is made with the coagulated matter from the whey of cow's or sheep's milk, which is "recooked" (Ricotta means recooked). It has therefore tended to flourish in the shadow of *grand cru* cheeses. Val d'Aoste and Piedmont Ricotta are made from the whey left over from the production of Fontina, Fontal and Provolone. In the same way, Ricotta's equivalent in Savoie on the other side of the Alps, Sérac, is a by-product of Beaufort. The most popular Ricotta cheese

in central and southern Italy, RICOTTA ROMANA is made with sheep's milk. Ricotta is smoked in the Friuli region in the north-east, a method of preservation also found in the mountains of central Europe. The recipes for Apulian Ricotta, which is spicy and flavoured with herbs, and for Calabrian Ricotta, for which vegetable rennet (fig sap) is used to make the milk into curds, are as old as the civilisations in these regions.

Ricotta forms a key ingredient in a traditional kind of pie (a mix of Ricotta, orange and lemon peel and pine kernels). It is eaten with pasta, salads and meats and can even be put in the oven. The strength of its flavour varies according to whether it is made with cow's milk, sheep's milk or a mixture of both, and whether it is salted or smoked. It is drained in a mould or a basket which also serves to give it its shape.

Shepherd and shepherdess from the province of Abruzzi (LEFT). 19th-century engraving. *Bibliothèque des Arts Décoratifs, Paris.* BOTTOM LEFT: Provolone. BELOW: Ricotta-seller in Ligurian regional costume (1820).

Ricotta is a granular, soft, white, slightly acid-tasting cheese containing about 30% fat and 18% protein, but now that it has become an up-market product, unskimmed milk is sometimes added to it, which increases its fat content. Like any fresh food, Ricotta should be eaten quickly. The salted kind can be kept for up to 2 months.

Ricotta (RIGHT). CENTRE: Taleggio. TOP RIGHT: Mascarpone. BOTTOM RIGHT: Bel Paese. PRECEDING PAGES: sheep milking in Tuscany.

■ RICOTTA

Soft cheese made with sheep's or cow's milk or a mixture of both (up to 30% fat)

TYPE: soft, white; rindless

SHAPE: slab or large truncated cone

WEIGHT: 300 g to 3 kg

TALEGGIO

One of the oldest Lombardy cheeses, probably dating from the 9th century. Taleggio is another example of a cheese originally made using milk from cows stopping off at the small town of the same name in the province of Bergamo on their way back from

the mountains for the winter. 30 minutes after the rennet has been added, the curds are cut into walnut-sized pieces and put in a cloth to drain. They are then transferred to a mould and left to mature under cold (4° C) and humid conditions for 45 days. Sometimes the cheese is left to mature for longer, in which case its taste becomes stronger.

■ TALEGGIO

Cow's milk cheese (minimum 48% fat)

TYPE: soft, unpressed, straw coloured; thin, flexible, pinkish rind

SHAPE: rectangular block, 19 by 22 by 4 cm

WEIGHT: 1.7 to 2.2 kg

MATURATION: 40 days

OTHER CHEESES

MASCARPONE is a delicious soft cream cheese containing 70% fat. It is often eaten as a dessert cheese, sometimes accompanied by cognac, but it is also frequently used in the preparation of

certain dishes and sauces. Mascarpone is made in the winter in Lombardy. It is a very soft cheese and is sold pre-packed in pots or wrapped in gold paper. BEL PAESE, or "beautiful land" cheese first appeared in the same region. It was invented at the beginning of the century near Milan, and has been a great success with the gourmets. It is a soft cow's milk cheese containing 48% fat. The uncooked pressed cheese is soaked in brine, then matured for 45 days in a humid environment and washed regularly during that time. It is sold in rounds 20 cm in diameter and 4 to 5 cm thick, wrapped in silver paper and weighing 2 kg.

In the 5th millenium BC, the Iberian peninsula suffered the consequences of the drying up of the Sahara. Sheep and goats, which could make do with only meagre grazing land, were probably introduced to the region via the coast of North Africa, from Egypt and the Near East, from around the 4th millenium BC. Towards 1100 BC the Phoenecians, then the Greeks, began to settle along the coast and exchanges with the rest of the Mediterranean increased, while the Iberians, whose origins are obscure, but may lie in North Africa, moved into the interior of the peninsula.

The Romans invaded the country in the 1st century BC. Traces of the vast domains given to Roman legionnaires in return for a good and loyal service are still visible in the huge farms of Andalucia even today and some of the remotest ancestors of Spanish cheeses no doubt lie in the Roman Empire. The great transhumances of central Spain were already established in the 4th century. They were not disturbed by either the fall of the Empire or the long Moslem occupation (8th to 15th century), and the attendant conflicts of the Reconquest undertaken by the Catholic Kings. The flocks of sheep spent the winter in Extremadura in the north-west, and in the south of Castile, and the summer in the high mountains of the north.

In 1526 the country's livestock herds contained 3.5 million animals. The owners of small herds were associated with a guild, the *mesta,* which enjoyed crown protection, since much of the royal income came from wool sold abroad. The growth of the cotton market in the 17th century brought an end to the wool trade, but the herds were kept up for their milk. The Moslems passed their taste for soft sheep's and goat's cheeses on to the Spanish. Cheese was not just a food for the peasants, but also for the hard-up, country-dwelling minor nobility who could not often afford to buy meat, which was scarce and expensive.

Heading an impressive list of 100 or so Spanish cheeses, surprisingly varied, and displaying a diversity of shapes and striking patterns stamped on to the cheeses in relief, comes Manchego, from the vast plains of New Castile, with their icy winters and scorching hot summers.

The great cow's milk cheeses come from the Balearic Islands, where the English established cattle-rearing when they settled in Minorca following the signing of the Utrecht Treaty in 1713. To improve the milk yield of their herds, the English introduced cattle from Italy, and so were able to begin using the milk to make cheese. This cheese was apparently "more highly prized than Parmesan" and was exported to Italy. Since the 1970s, Spain has set up a system of certification of origin (AOC) to enhance the value of its great

At the entrance to Toledo (ABOVE). Ceramic tile wall-decoration. BOTTOM: a shepherd and his flock near the village of Guadix in Andalucia.

cheeses. On the other hand, it must not be forgotten that the wealth of Spanish cheeses owes as much to all the local produce from the old rural communities, still so important in a country which remains so largely rural.

CABRALES

A grain loft in Villanueva near Oiredo in the Asturias (BOTTOM). FAR RIGHT: Cabrales.

Cabrales is a rustic blue cheese from the Asturias in northern Spain. The secret of its maturation lies in the cool damp draughts which are passed through the attics where it is put to ripen. There are still a number of villages clinging to the rocky slopes of the Picos de Europa, overlooking the Gulf of Gascony, which make this cheese, whose taste is as rough and ready as the lives of the peasants of the region. The latter rear cattle, sheep and goats in the Concejo de Cabrales valley, grazing them on the high mountain pastures in the summer months. The AOC applies to about 150 small cottage-industry producers, who do not make much of a living from

this blue cheese, with its strongly earthy taste. Paradoxically, one of the characteristics of this AOC is the diversity of the milk sources used, which in no way detracts from its quality. According to the seasons, it may be made with cow's, goat's or sheep's milk, or a mixture of milks. This means that the cheese may be mild, pungent or strong, the best being made in the springtime with milk from the mountain pastures.

The morning's milk, mixed with that of the previous evening, is heated to 30° C, if the chill of the season demands it. Otherwise it is used at room temperature. Coagulation, which is precipitated by means of calves' or sheeps' rennet or even by the use of chemicals (more and more frequently), can take several hours. The curds are left to stand for a while before being strained into moulds, called *arnios*, for 24 hours. The cheeses are then dry-salted every day on each side alternately, changing moulds each time they are salted. They are then left in a cool, airy place for 3 weeks, and turned over regularly. The most important stage in the maturation process takes place in damp caves in the mountains, or, failing that, in attics, where the cheeses, kept at a temperature

of 4 to 12° C over 3 months, become impregnated naturally with *Penicillium glaucum*, and gradually grow a mould. Cabrales used to be wrapped in plane leaves to absorb its "sweating". Now that it has been promoted to the rank of an AOC, and is distributed to places far from where it is made, it is sold wrapped in a sheet of silver paper with the brand label marked on it.

■ CABRALES

Cheese made from sheep's, goat's or cow's milk, or a mixture (45% fat)

TYPE: semi-hard, creamy, white with blue-green streaks; thin, fragile, greyish rind, pinkish in places

SHAPE: cylinder 7 to 15 cm tall

WEIGHT: 2 to 6 kg

PRESENTATION: wrapped in silver paper

CANTABRIA

This is an AOC cheese made on the territory of the autonomous community of Cantábrico (comprising the valleys cf the Urdon and the Cervera) in the province of Santander.

This region, swept by wet winds from the Gulf of Gascony, keeps herds of Friesian cattle, whose unskimmed and pasteurised milk yields a cheese which s matured for only a few days.

■ CANTABRIA

Friesian cow's milk cheese

(minimum 45% fat)

TYPE: semi-hard, ivory; soft yellow rind

SHAPE: rectangular block or cylinder

WEIGHT: 1 to 2 kg

MATURATION: 7 days

IDIAZABAL

This AOC Basque cheese is produced in the provinces of Alava, Guipuzcoa and Vizcaya. It is made from the summer milk of Lacha and Carranzana sheep which graze in the mountains. The urpasteurised milk is made into curds using natural rennet, then broken up into small pieces. These are placed

into cylindrical moulds, then pressed. Next the cheese is salted using coarse salt, or immersed in brine, for 2 days. The maturation generally takes 2 months in a cool damp cellar, but it can take longer. The cheeses are turned over and brushed regularly. Idiazabal is made on small farms and was traditionally hung up in chimneys so that it became impregnated with the smell of the woodsmoke.

This custom has been retained: about ten days before they are put on sale, the cheeses are smoked over beech and hawthorn wood, which gives them their very distinctive aroma and taste, and turns the rind to dark brown. URBIA, ENTZIA, GORBEA and ORDUNA cheeses are close relatives of Idiazabal and also have protected names and legally defined production areas.

■ IDIAZABAL

Lacha and Carranzana sheep's milk

cheese (minimum 45% fat)

TYPE: semi-hard, dense, ivory; hard,

pale yellow (unsmoked) or dark

brown (smoked) rind

SHAPE: cylinder

WEIGHT: 1 to 2 kg

MATURATION: 2 months minimum

LIEBANA PICON

Liebana is made on the eastern side of the Picos de Europa, which has a temperate microclimate, allowing vines and olives to be grown there. There are several varieties of this cheese, made with cow's, sheep's or goat's milk, or a mixture. Liebana Picon is made from these three milks, either alone or in combination. The curds are cut into 1 or 2 cm cubes. The cheese matures in 2 months and looks very like Cabrales with the same blue-green moulds running through it, its soft, greasy, grey rind and its wrapping of plane leaves.

Cantabria (FAR LEFT).

TOP: Idiazabal.

BELOW: a large flock of sheep near Sépulveda in the Segovia region.

SMOKED LIEBANA is made from unskimmed cow's milk. The curds are broken up into tiny morsels. The cheese is matured for 2 months and smoked over juniper wood. It is a round cheese measuring 10 to 20 cm across and 2 to 10 cm thick and weighing 500 g to 2 kg. QUESUCOS is also a Liebana. It is eaten either unripe or just ripened. The unripe cheese is made from pasteurised cow's, sheep's or goat's milk. The ripe version is made from unpasteurised milk and takes 2 months to mature. The cheese is sold in small rounds weighing 100 to 500 g.

Aerial view of a farm in Minorca (TOP).
BOTTOM: Liebana Picon.

■ LIEBANA PICON

Unskimmed sheep's, goat's or cow's milk, singly or combined (45% fat)

TYPE: white, streaked with blue-green veins; soft grey rind

SHAPE: cylinder 30 cm in diameter, 7 to 15 cm tall

WEIGHT: 1 to 5 kg

MATURATION: 2 months minimum

MAHON

This cheese comes from the Balearic Islands, which served as a commercial base for the Phoenicians and Greeks, who introduced sheep to the archipelago. Cheese was therefore already being produced there in classical times. Renaissance chroniclers refer to sales of sheep's cheeses, pointing out that they were offered as gifts to important visitors. Mahon originated on Minorca, and is named after its capital. At the end of the last century, Mahon played an important role in the barter economy between traders and peasants, who paid for the goods they bought with fresh cheeses. The "collectors" then matured these cheeses and exported them. In 1930, a business was set up in Minorca with the aim of collecting the best part of the production and Mahon gradually attained a consistent level of quality, backed up by detailed rules of hygiene. Mahon was first made with cow's milk after the English introduced good dairy breeds to the island. Nowadays it is made almost entirely from this milk, whether pasteurised or unpasteurised, with the proportion of sheep's milk not allowed to exceed 5%.

After each milking, the milk is put with animal rennet at a temperature of 30 to 37° C. After 30 to 40 minutes, the curds are broken into little pieces, then wrapped in a sturdy linen or cotton cloth which serves as a mould and gives the cheese its shape. This cloth, called a *fogasser,* is also used to press the cheese, the four corners of the cloth being folded over the cheese and pegged together. The cheese is then pressed, first by hand, and then using a press worked by a lever, for 10 to 14 hours. The marks left on the cheese by the cloth are called *mamella.* The maturation, which includes regular washes, goes on for between 2 months and a year. After 1 month of maturation, Mahon is sometimes coated with butter or virgin olive oil perfumed with paprika.

■ MAHON

Cow's milk cheese, sometimes
containing a maximum of 5% goat's milk
(minimum 45% fat)

TYPE: semi-hard, ivory yellow, unevenly
distributed holes; dense brownish
yellow rind

SHAPE: round-cornered slab
8 to 9 cm thick

WEIGHT: 1 to 4 kg

MATURATION: 2 months (semi-young),
5 months (semi-mature), 10 months
(mature)

MANCHEGO

"In a corner of the Mancha, whose
name I cannot recall, there lived a
hidalgo." Thus did Miguel de Cervantes
begin his epic account of Don Quixote
in 1605. In the course of the
peregrinations of his "Knight of the
Sorrowful Countenance" the author
reveals details of the life of the
peasants of his period, making

a passing reference to the numerous
herds of goats and sheep whose milk
yielded a cheese "harder than if it had
been made out of sand and lime". This
was his description of Manchego, the
Spanish cheese best known outside
Spain. Manchego originated on the vast
plain, grazed by the hardy Manchega
breed of sheep, which stretches across
the provinces of Ciudad Real, Albacete,
Cuenca and Toledo.

The cheese is both made and matured
in this region, which is the sole holder
of the rights to the AOC. It is made
with sheep's milk – pasteurised
or unpasteurised – and natural rennet.
The coagulation takes less than an
hour at a temperature of 28 to 32° C.
The curds are then broken into pieces
the size of a large pea, and reheated
to 40° C. Next the cheese is placed
in cylindrical moulds which print
embossed images of traditional moulds

made of straw, flowers and plaiting
into the cheese. This is then taken out
of the mould, then either dry-salted
by hand or placed in brine.

MANCHEGO CURADO is matured for at
least 2 months, guaranteed by its AOC.
"OLD" MANCHEGO is matured for
9 to 12 months in a damp cellar. During
this period the rind is washed.

Manchego can also be prepared
in "aceite": that is, soaked in olive oil,
which gives it a very dark coloration.
Manchego is the best-known of
a series of similar sheep's cheeses,
which may be fresh or mature, and are
marked with traditional motifs picked
out in relief. Among these are
ZAMORANO (from Zamora, to the north-
east of Madrid), CADIZ, ARACENA (from
the Andalucian province of Huelva),
CALAHORA (from around Granada) and
CASTELLENO (from the province of Léon).

■ MANCHEGO

Manchega sheep's milk cheese (57% fat)

TYPE: hard, ivory white to yellow

Manchego (ABOVE).

TOP LEFT: Mahon.

BOTTOM: courtyard of
the Santa-Cruz Palace
in Toledo. LEFT: olive
oil-soaked Manchego.

Label for "Flor de Esgueva" cheese (ABOVE), made from sheep's milk in Penafiel (Valladolid province). CENTRE: Roncal. BELOW: a farm in Urdax, typical of the Pamplona region.

depending on maturity; hard rind, pale yellow to grey green, or black with motifs picked out in relief showing plaiting and flowers

SHAPE: round, 25 cm in diameter, 10 cm thick

WEIGHT: 2 to 3.5 kg

MATURATION: up to 1 year depending on the type of Manchego

RONCAL

Roncal is made from the milk of Lacha and Rasa sheep. Its production zone is limited to the seven valleys which make up the large Ronca region, in the province of Navarra. Milk produced between December and July is used unskimmed to make it. Coagulation using natural rennet takes 1 hour at 32 to 37° C. The curds are broken into rice-grain sized fragments and stirred and beaten to force the whey out more quickly. Once it has been moulded and

pressed, the cheese is either dry-salted or placed in brine. Roncal with an AOC is matured in a cool cellar for at least 4 months, during which time it is turned over and washed frequently.

■ RONCAL

Cheese made from the unskimmed milk of Rasa and Lacha sheep (under 50% fat)

TYPE: hard, small irregular holes, yellowish white; thick, hard rind, straw coloured or brown, with traditional motifs picked out in relief

SHAPE: round, 8 to 12 cm thick

WEIGHT: 2 to 3 kg

MATURATION: 4 months minimum

OTHER CHEESES

MALLORQUIN is a semi-hard cow's or sheep's milk cheese, made in Majorca, with a red rind. In Gran Canaria they make a slightly soft, round, cow's or sheep's milk cheese with a reddish rind called FLOR DE GUIA. Native to Tenerife is a round semi-hard cheese made from cow's, sheep's or goat's

milk called TENERIFE. CONEJERO, a washed cheese from Lanzarote in the Canaries, and MAJORERO, from the island of Fuerteventura, are two goat's milk cheeses.

Many of the sheep's milk cheeses made on the mainland deserve a mention here. For example, although Andalucia has not been credited with any AOC cheeses, an astonishing variety of specialities are made there. ALHAMA and CALAHORA, a little-matured cheese, shaped into a thick round with a seal of Solomon printed in relief on the rind, are two such cheeses from Granada. Some curiously-shaped soft cheeses are produced in Alicante, among them SERVILETTA which, like Mahon, is kept in a cloth for part of its maturation, so that the cloth leaves its marks on the cheese, and NUCIA, which is made in the form of a truncated cone decorated with embossed lozenges. From further north, in the province of Léon, comes a cheese called ARMADA, whose stud-covered cylindrical form, reminiscent of a suit of armour, justifies the evocation of the age of the conquistadores in its name.

The Asturias, Galicia and Extremadura also produce quality sheep's cheeses, but they are not sold much outside the regions in which they are made.

As early as the 15th century, Portugal had established itself as a major maritime power, but while the coast and the large cities benefited from the colonial expansion and grew rich on the gold, spices and sugar trades, the high plateaus of the interior remained closed off in a longstanding autarky. To a certain extent, these regions have been able to keep their traditions free of outside influences. Their cheeses, most of which are made with sheep's milk, and some with goat's milk, have also retained their distinctive character. One aspect of this is the use of vegetable-based rennet, rather than the traditional calves' rennet, which is used only rarely. Most of the cheese is still made in cottage industries or small-scale cooperatives.

The producers of the Serra da Estrela region have formed a group to ensure that the quality and originality of their QUEIJO DA SERRA cheese is maintained. But they are the only instance of this sort of organisation and there is a risk that dairy-made cheeses may wipe out these locally made cheeses, as small producers find it more profitable to sell their milk to the industrial dairies, which make cheeses in the style of Edam, Emmental or Camembert.

AZEITÃO

This small round sheep's milk cheese resembles unripe Serra. It is made in the Setubal region south of Lisbon, a very hot plain, which explains the fact that it is matured for a shorter period than most other Portuguese cheeses.

■ AZEITÃO

Sheep's milk cheese (45 to 55% fat)

TYPE: semi-hard, dense, white or very pale yellow;

SHAPE: small, rounded, 7.5 to 9 cm in diameter, 3.5 to 4.5 cm thick

WEIGHT: about 250 g

MATURATION: 20 days

CASTELO BRANCO

This sheep's or goat's milk cheese is named after the canton to the south of the Serra de Estrela where it is made. Its characteristics are similar to those of Queijo da Serra. Sheep's milk Castelo Branco takes 40 days to mature. If left to mature for longer it becomes harder.

Castelo Branco made with goat's milk is a soft cheese made at the end of the autumn and sold after 10 days' maturation. If matured for longer, this cheese develops a stronger taste. It is also sometimes made according to another method which produces a very pungent, creamy, rindless cheese. In this case, it is left to mature for 8 days, and thereafter coated in ash and scraped regularly over a 3 month period to prevent any mould from forming.

■ CASTELO BRANCO

Sheep's or goat's milk cheese (45 to 50% fat)

TYPE: soft, white to straw coloured; firm, straw coloured rind

Portrait of a Portuguese man with the essential nutriments (BOTTOM): bread, wine, and cheese. Anonymous painting. *The Louvre, Paris.* CENTRE: Azeitão.

SHAPE: small round, 14 to 15 cm in diameter, 5 to 6 cm thick

WEIGHT: 1.15 kg (sheep's cheese) to 1.5 kg (goat's cheese)

MATURATION: 40 days or more (sheep's cheese), 10 days or more (goat's cheese), 3 1/2 months (strong goat's cheese)

ILHA DO PICO

Portugal was the first European country to embark on the conquest of the Atlantic and to fly its flag on the island of Madeira and the Azores. All Portuguese cow's milk cheese comes from these islands. While Madeira has a Mediterranean climate, the cool, wet climate of the Azores is well-suited to cattle-rearing. The pastures are small fields enclosed by low walls.

ILHA SÃO JORGE cheese, made on the little island of São Jorge, is a distant relation of English Cheddar, whose production methods were probably

Goats in the mountain region of Serra da Estrela (BELOW). TOP: Ilha do Pico.

imported into the Azores via maritime through-traffic in the last century. The cheese is also made, though in smaller quantities, on the other islands. It is exported to Lisbon and North America. Ilha São Jorge is a hard, granular cheese, made with unpasteurised cow's milk containing 45 to 50% fat. It is made in large rounds, weighing 5 to 10 kg and measuring 30 to 35 cm in diameter and 10 to 20 cm in thickness. It has a strong smell and a pungent taste. Less reminiscent of Cheddar and more typically Portuguese is Ilha do Pico, made on the island of São Pico, which features the highest peak of the Azores, Mount Pico (2351 m). This soft smooth cheese, made from unpasteurised cow's milk sometimes mixed with goat's milk, is a local adaptation of Serra cheese.

■ ILHA DO PICO

Unpasteurised cow's milk cheese (45 to 55% fat)

TYPE: hard and granular, very pale yellow;

hard, smooth, straw coloured rind

SHAPE: small round, 9 cm in diameter, 3 cm thick

WEIGHT: about 500 g

SERRA

Mountain cheeses, or "queijos da serra", are the traditional Portuguese sheep's cheeses, made since time immemorial by shepherds and smallholders in the mountainous regions. The Serra da Estrela, in the centre of the country, which reaches almost 2000 m in altitude, is home to a cheese of the same name which enjoys an AOC status. Several cantons in the regions of Guarda and Coimbra, and a number of neighbouring districts also produce similar varieties. Sheep's milk from the Serra da Estrela is clotted using *Cynara cardunculus* flowers or leaves, a thistle which grows in arid mountain areas, and is sold on market stalls. This serves as a natural rennet substitute for calves' rennet in this region, where there are no cattle. The cheese is entirely hand-made, in the literal sense of the term, as the curds are broken up by hand and not cut up with an implement as is usually the case. The maturation, which takes 30 to 40 days, is done in two stages: the first part in damp cellars or caves, and the second in very dry cold cellars or caves. It may be extended over several months, in which case the cheese is harder, stronger tasting and smooth-rinded. Several other mountain cheeses merit a mention here. SERPA, or ALENTEJO made around Beja, a mountainous area to the east of the Alentejo, is related to Serra cheese and of a similar size and consistency, although slightly more fatty, more pungent and stronger flavoured. ALCOBACA is a sheep's milk mountain cheese, sometimes containing some cow's milk. NIZA is another cheese made in the mountains, using either sheep's or goat's milk.

■ SERRA

Sheep's milk cheese (45% fat)

TYPE: soft, sometimes holed; hard, sometimes cracked rind, pale yellow

SHAPE: small round, 16 to 18 cm in diameter, 6 to 7.5 cm thick

WEIGHT: 1.5 to 2 kg

MATURATION: minimum 30 days

OTHER CHEESES

Portugal makes a large number of small, very hard, salted, disc-shaped goat's cheeses. such as EVORA DE L'ALENTEJO. These usually weigh about 100 g and take a year to mature. Several very small sheep's cheeses, weighing 40 g or less, with a fat content of 50 to 55% are sold in the regions where they are made. An example of these is SALOIO a small round cheese, 6 cm in diameter and 2 cm thick, made near Lisbon, and sold without having been matured. Another is TOMAR, which is a semi-hard cheese, 5 cm in diameter and 2 cm thick, made in the upper Tagus. Until this cheese production was regulated, the same cheese was frequently made with different milks, mixed or unmixed, according to what

was available. Thus, ALVERCA a soft or semi-hard cheese from the Ribatejo, may be made from either sheep's or goat's milk. It contains 40 to 50% fat and weighs 100 g or more.

RABACAL a fresh cheese made using sheep's and goat's milk, with a very high fat content (50 to 60%), exists in various sizes but never weighs more than 1 kg. It is sold a few days after it is made and it is then up to the purchaser to decide how much longer to let it ripen, whether to eat it soft or semi-hard.

Herds on a farm in Alentejo, to the south of the Taga (TOP). BOTTOM LEFT: Serra. LEFT: view of Lisbon.

Cheese was a food fit for the pharaohs, and featured among the delicacies left in their tombs to accompany them on their journey to the land of the dead. Cows, sheep and goats often appear in funeral-chamber paintings. Nowadays, Egypt produces a wide range of cheeses. KAREISH is made from whey strained through cloth, salted, then sliced and either eaten fresh or preserved in brine. BEDA and

A fresco discovered in 1922 in the tomb of Tutankhamen in the Valley of Kings, in Egypt (RIGHT). TOP: goats grazing on miserable land in the Algerian Sahara, watched over by Touareg shepherds. BELOW: nomads of the Mauritanian desert. CENTRE: a not unusual sight in the Moroccan desert: goats perched in trees, the leaves of which provide essential nourishment lacking on the otherwise barren land. BOTTOM RIGHT: Sardo.

MISCH are made using skimmed milk, the former being matured in whey, and the latter in salted and spiced milk. RUMI whose name (meaning Roman or European) reveals its origins, is a semi-hard cheese, similar to Gouda.

First colonisation, then emigration, led to an increase in the consumption of cheese in north-west Africa. Up until independence, most cheeses made

there were imitations of Mediterranean produce. For example: SICILE, a round cheese with a hard rind, flavoured with paprika and weighing between 5 and 10 kg, SARDO, a hard, long-lasting sheep's cheese, often used for grating, and TESTOURI, shaped like an orange, similar to Lebenen and very common in the Near East, introduced into North

Africa by the Ottomans after the 15th century. Made from beaten milk, this cheese is eaten fresh and lightly salted. However, cheese production is virtually non-existent here today. In Mauritania, where the climate precludes the production of hard cheese, the only dairy product other than milk is ZRIG, made with beaten and fermented goat's and camel's milk, which may or may not be sweetened. In the central Sahara, the Touaregs make a skimmed-milk cheese. The curds are formed by adding vegetable rennet, and strained using cloth or dried grasses. The cheese soon hardens in the hot dry climate.

The food of shepherds, cheese was also the food of the Greek gods, who did not scorn contact with mortals. While goat's milk was the drink of the children of the gods, curds were the food of heroes such as Heracles, who was offered soft cheeses by the islanders of Kos. Greek mythology abounds with references to milk and cheese. Moreover, it depicts an eminently pastoral world, where gods, goddesses and nymphs dwell among animals, drinking their milk and wearing their fur. The presiding god in this arcadia was Pan, half goat, half man, the protector of shepherds and their flocks, carrying his crook in one hand and his pipes in the other. Cheese made its appearance in the menus of Greek cuisine very early on. Cheese-drainers have been found on sites from the Archaic period (10th-6th centuries BC). Cheese had its place at banquets held in honour of the gods and mythical heroes, where it was served with savoury cakes, olives and leeks. It is mentioned by the Spartan Lycurgus (3rd century BC), who recommends that citizens eat collective meals consisting of oil, flour, honey, fruit and cheese. Homer provides the first detailed description of cheese-making when he relates Ulysses' captivity in the cave of the Cyclops, Polyphemus. The terrible monster leaves his sheep's milk to clot, then tranfers it to baskets of woven rushes to strain off the whey. These little round baskets are still used around the Mediterranean, from Spain to the Levant.

FETA

The production of Feta can certainly be traced back as far as antiquity, and probably further still. Over the centuries, this cheese, which is still eaten by the peasants of Mani, has spread its appeal throughout the world. Until quite recently, Greek shepherds continued to make Feta according to traditional methods. After milking, the milk was poured into a goatskin or other receptacle containing the remains of the previous day's curds. When mixed with this, the fresh milk soon clotted. Other means of clotting included beating the milk with a freshly-cut fig branch, whose sap served as rennet, or soaking thistle-flowers in it. In modern dairies, the milk is coagulated at 35° C, and the curds are broken up then placed in perforated wooden or tin moulds. After being strained and pressed for 24 hours, the cheese is cut into large slices (*feta* means slice in Greek), which

are transferred to wooden barrels or, more often these days, into steel churns, filled with brine. The Feta is ready to eat after a month. If matured for longer it develops a stronger flavour. More or less salted according to taste, Feta is the essence of the Greek salad. The Greeks prefer a perfectly white, smooth Feta made from sheep's milk, although cow's or goat's milk is sometimes added.

The cream-coloured cow's milk Feta is less sought after. Being easy to make, it is produced in several countries, but there is nothing to match a good Greek Feta made from milk scented with the most quintessentially Mediterranean fragrances. TOULCUMISIO is a variety of Feta macerated in wooden barrels, then in a brine-filled goatskin. It is left to mature for several months.

■ FETA
Sheep's milk cheese (45% fat), cow's milk cheese, or a mixture including goat's milk

Feta (TOP).
BELOW: label from a Greek soft cheese.

TYPE: soft, white (sheep's milk), yellow
(cow's milk); rindless

SHAPE: chunky bread-roll

MATURATION: at least 1 month, in brine

KEFALOTYRI

This is a relatively recent cheese
compared to Feta, dating back only
a few centuries. Its name comes from
the *kefalo,* the Greek hat whose shape
it evokes. It is made all over Greece,
taking the name of every region in
which it is produced. This
unpasteurised goat's or sheep's milk
cheese, whose fat content varies, is
pressed in a mould then salted and
pressed again. It is matured in a cool,
humid cellar for 2 to 3 months. Certain
more mature cheeses become harder
and are used for grating.
KASSERI is a young Kefalotyri, whose
consistency is made more elastic

A Greek peasant
drying his cheeses
along the wall of his
farm (BELOW).
TOP: Kefalotyri.
FAR RIGHT: Manouri.
OPPOSITE: a Cretan
shepherd with his
goats at milking time,
on the Lassithi plateau.

by immersion in hot water. It is sold
in small discs or bars.

■ KEFALOTYRI
Sheep's or goat's milk cheese
(up to 45% fat)
TYPE: pressed, semi-hard; dry rind
SHAPE: rounded (like the kefalo hat),
25 cm thick
WEIGHT: 10 kg
MATURATION: 2 to 3 months
in a cool cellar.

OTHER CHEESES
Whey from Feta or Kefalotyri is used
to produce a delicious "poor man's"
cheese which, unlike other cheeses
of this type, such as the Norwegian
Gjetost, is eaten fresh.
Like Feta, GALOTYRI is one of the oldest
Greek cheeses, but it remains a local
product, since its production is hard
to adapt to industrial processes. After
standing for about an hour, the milk
is boiled, salted, then curdled. It is then
beaten several times and strained

before being mixed with the curds
of the original cheeses in a goatskin,
the traditional receptacle of nomadic
shepherds. Maturation takes between
2 and 3 months.
Many cheeses bear the name of their
native region or island. SKYROS, a semi-
hard cheese similar to Kefalotyri,
comes from the island of Skyros, while
SALAMANA soft sheep's milk cheese
matured in a goatskin is produced around
Salamis. MANOURI a soft goat's or sheep's

milk cheese, is shaped like a truncated
cone. KOPANISTI, a blue cheese from the
Cyclades, is made with unpasteurised
goat's or sheep's milk, sometimes both
together. In the past, the milk for this
cheese used to be left to curdle naturally,
without adding rennet. The curds are
kneaded into balls which are placed on a
rack where they quickly become covered
in mould. Once they have been kneaded
again and salted, the balls are kept in
a pot covered with a cloth, where they
mature over several months.

This large, mountainous island with its Mediterranean climate, more humid in the north than in the south, has been populated since the 7th millenium BC. Between 3000 BC and 1000 BC, it spawned the brilliant Minoan civilisation, whose legendary judge and sovereign, King Minos of Knossos, has been perpetuated by Greek mythology. This land of olive trees, vines, cereal crops

and sheep-rearing, offers a range of produce similar to that of its larger neighbour. Almost all the cheeses of main and Greece and the Cyclades can be found here. MITZITHRA, a soft goat's or sheep's milk cheese is left to dry in the open air, wrapped in muslin. GRAVIERA, the equivalent of Gruyère, is served as a dessert cheese, but also used in pastries. Several varieties of this cheese are produced in different regions. KRITIKO (Cretan) is a hard sheep's milk cheese made by shepherds, and exported throughout Greece.

Mitzithra being drained in muslin bags; an effective though somewhat archaic method (RIGHT). TOP CENTRE: goat's milk Kashkaval at Limassol market in Cyprus. FAR RIGHT: maturation, wrapped in straw, of the Cypriot cheese, Anari. BOTTOM: goats in the Nikokhia countryside in Cyprus.

The population of this eastern Mediterranean island is divided between Greeks (with a majority of about 75%) and Turks. First inhabited in the 7th millenium BC, it functioned as a major trading centre for the Aegean, Syria and Egypt throughout antiquity. Its rich seams of copper gave the metal its name and it was exported throughout the Mediterranean from the 3rd century BC. The island has a particularly turbulent

history. Domination by the Ptolemeans and the Romans was followed by conquest or administration by the Byzantines and the Arabs, the crusaders of Richard the Lionheart, the Genoese, Venetians, Turks and British. Some of the traditional cheeses of the region are of course found there, such as FETA and KASKAVALI, a close relation of Bulgarian Katschkawalj and of Italian Caciocavallo. But there is also HALLOUMI,

a sheep's or goat's milk cheese and ANARI a soft sheep's or goat's cheese matured in attractive plaited moulds.

The Ottoman Empire reigned for centuries over the Levant and North Africa. This glorious era gave rise to a rich civilisation whose renowned cuisine still forms a link between east and west. In central and eastern Turkey, the continental climate – very hot in the summer, freezing in winter – is well-suited to breeding Angora sheep and Anatolian long-haired goats, which produce high-quality milk. Curdled milk, the staple diet of the nomads, is consumed fresh, there being no cheese-making in the strict sense of the term. On the Aegean and Black Sea coasts, where the climate is milder, hard cheeses of several months' maturation are produced, as well as Beyaz, a soft white cheese stored in brine, which forms part of the basic diet of the smallholders.

BEYAZ PEYNIR

Peynir is Turkish for cheese, but the word mostly designates the commonest cheese, Beyaz Peynir, or "cheese of the Bey". Like Greek Feta, Beyaz is a sheep's milk cheese found throughout European Turkey. Carefully filtered milk is clotted using vegetable rennet in the small farms, or chemicals in the large dairies. The curds

are pressed for a few hours, then cut into pieces and strained again. Formerly matured in sheep- or goatskins, nowadays they are put in tin containers, salted layer by layer and covered with brine. Beyaz can be preserved thus for at least 6 months and must be desalinated before tasting.

■ BEYAZ PEYNIR

Sheep's milk cheese (45% fat)

TYPE: soft; rindless

SHAPE: thick slices

WEIGHT: about 500 g

MATURATION: preserved in brine.

MIHALIC

This hard sheep's milk cheese comes from the Bursa region in the Dardanelles. The milk is first curdled in a barrel, then divided into small portions, which are sprinkled with hot water and stirred. After being left to stand, the curds are strained by forcing the liquid out through a knotted cloth. The cheese that remains is cut into large slices, then salted and dried for 1 or 2 weeks, packed in containers with brine and left to mature for up to 3 months.

■ MIHALIC

Sheep's milk cheese (45% fat)

TYPE: firm; moist rind

SHAPE: thick slices

WEIGHT: 500 g to 1 kg

MATURATION: 2 to 3 months preserved in lightly salted water.

A hooded Turkish shepherd on the road from Bergama to Bursa in Turkey (ABOVE). TOP: Beyaz Peynir. BOTTOM: the ancient town of Bursa nestling in the foothills of Mount Olympus.

OTHER CHEESES

Could KASAR be the cheese of the Kazakhs, the nomadic tribe who came from Central Asia at the time of the great invasions? Kasar Peynir is a hard or semi-hard pressed sheep's milk cheese (sometimes also cow's or goat's milk). It can be eaten fresh and weighs around 2 kg.

Shepherd and flock wandering over ancient ruins in Turkey (BELOW). RIGHT: Kasar. TOP RIGHT: goats by Lake Tiberias (the Sea of Gallilee). FAR RIGHT: Akawi, a soft white cheese packed in brine, also used desalinated in sweet pastries .

TULUM is one of many Turkish cheeses made in a cloth or skin pouch. This pressed cheese, with its strong tangy taste, is strained in a large suspended cloth, then beaten. The curds are broken up, salted, and pressed in a goatskin, where the cheese matures for a few months.

The Israelis eat a great deal of cheese. As in all the eastern Mediterranean countries, the climate and the nomadic origins of the culture ensured that fresh cheeses and sour or curdled milk were dominant in the past. Following the war, the arrival of the Jews from Europe and the Arab countries brought the development of modern agriculture, and with it, the creation of a cheese-making industry. Dairies now produce imitations of European cheeses for consumption at home and abroad, among them CAMEMBERT, BRIE, EMMENTAL, GOUDA and PROVOLONE. Judaism forbids its followers to eat meat and dairy products in the same meal. Furthermore, cheese must be produced according to certain rules, which specifically proscribe the use of animal rennet or of dishes and utensils which have touched meat. Kosher cheese is therefore produced for local consumption and, increasingly, for the communities living abroad.

The Arab population uses several traditional cheeses, such as GWINA ZFATIT, a sheep's milk cheese sold in pots.

LEBBENE

Both the nomadic Arabs and the sedentary Jews have always eaten Lebbene fresh, dried or preserved in olive oil, as in the Lebanon and Syria (where it is known as Duberki). It won over the Israeli settlers who arrived after the war and is often served at breakfast with cucumber.

■ LEBBENE

Sheep's or goat's milk cheese
(minimum 45% fat)

TYPE: soft to firm

SHAPE: small balls

WEIGHT: 100 g

MATURATION: eaten young, almost liquid,
or in balls (Duberki) dried or preserved
in olive oil seasoned with herbs

A cheese shaped into small balls and often known as LEBENEN is made in a similiar fashion almost everywhere in the Middle East. It is also called LEBNEY in Syria, LABANEH in Jordan and GIBNE in the Arabian peninsula. The milk of a goat, sheep, camel, or occasionally a cow, is left to go sour for a day in a goatskin. It is then shaken in a sort of churn to separate the butter from the curds, which are strained using cotton cloth,

salted and rolled into little lumps the size of table-tennis balls. These may be matured in jars filled with olive oil and aromatic herbs. Jordanian Labaneh is made from soured cow's milk, to which

a little powdered milk is added. To make Lebney, the Bedouins of Syrian Jordan boil sour milk with cereals, then leave the mixture for 20 to 36 hours. After draining off the whey, they knead the cheese into little balls, adding aromatic herbs. These small cheeses are preserved in pots of olive oil. The little LEBANESE HALLOUMI is a soft sheep's milk cheese, eaten variously as an accompaniment to main courses and salads, or grilled on a skewer

Lebney preserved in jars of oil and aromatic herbs (FAR LEFT).

TOP CENTRE: Chuncliche, a highly spiced cheese rolled in thyme and sesame seeds. Typically eaten as a salad, combined with tomatoes and drenched in olive oil.

TOP RIGHT: Majdouhi, a fresh *pasta filata* type cheese. LEFT: Halloumi.

BOTTOM LEFT: goats in the oasis town of Palmyra, between Damascus and the Euphrates in Syria.

FOLLOWING PAGES: Iranian Quashgai women looking after their goats.

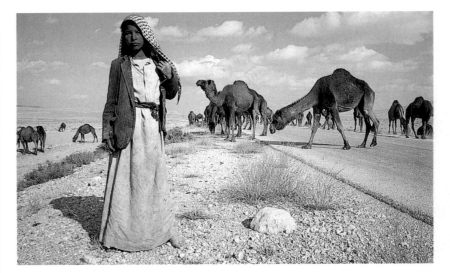

Since the development of the petroleum industry in Iraq, agriculture and stock-breeding no longer represent the nation's primary activity and cheese-making has suffered as a consequence. Among the traditional cheeses, the sheep's milk MEIRA is worth mentioning. The curds are strained in a cloth onto which a weight has been placed. They are then cut into strips and matured in a sheepskin bag for between 6 and 12 months before being sold at market. Other cheeses of interest include the ball-shaped ROOS, which is matured in a sheepskin bag and LOUR, a soft cheese made from whey and fresh milk. In the vast desert to the south of the Fertile Crescent, the Bedouins live on sheep's, goat's and camel's milk. In the cool season the semi-settled nomads make a small flattish cheese called JUPNEH, which is either eaten fresh or preserved in salt water. In ancient Babylon cheese was much more than a simple stomach-filler: it was a noble food, symbol of the domestication of nature and man's accession to civilisation. Babylonian banquets have passed into legend but one sheep's milk delicacy has remained, probably from the earliest times, known as BIZA or FAJY. This thin cheese is eaten fresh with onions and crushed garlic.

A Bedouin in the desert with his herd of camels (TOP). BELOW: Lour. BOTTOM: a herd of goats in Afghanistan. FAR RIGHT: Feta-style cheese.

The high mountains of Iran and Afghanistan were crossed 2500 years ago by caravans travelling the silk route, which brought camels to the region. The inhabitants of the lowlands depended on their orchards, whose fruits they dried for the winter, and on their herds of goats and sheep, source of meat, clothing and milk. The camels of the caravans have been replaced by lorries, but goats, sheep and she-camels continue to provide milk and cheese for the people. SERAT is made with sun-soured sheep's

milk. The curds are kneaded into a ball before being smoked and dipped in wax to preserve the cheese. The famous KADCHGALL cheese, mentioned by so many travellers, Marco Polo

among them, is mainly made from sheep's milk, but sometimes from camel's milk clotted with yoghurt. This cylindrical hard cheese weighs several kilos. The nomads skim the milk to make butter and use the skimmed milk to create cheeses reminiscent of Greek Feta, which they preserve in brine-filled pots or pouches.

In Nepal and Tibet, the yak, an animal capable of living in very low temperatures at 3000 to 4000 m altitude, produces a milk similar to that of sheep. This is used for making butter while the whey makes fermented milk and small cheeses. These are moulded, pressed between two stones, then wind- and sun-dried. They keep well and have a strong taste, as does the butter, which is put in tea in this region. The cows of the Indian plains are unsuited to the climatic conditions of the Himalayas and food-aid programmes have attempted to introduce hardier European breeds, especially Tarentaise cattle, which are good milkers and are used to high altitudes. The yak is also bred for its milk and meat on the high plateaus of central Asia. In Mongolia, yak's milk is turned into carbonated drinks and small dried cheeses, while horse's milk, used sour (like the Turkish AIRAG and Russian KUMISS) is similar to Kefir. On the Pamir plateau bactrian camels provide milk that the nomads turn into Chambat, an acidic drink, impregnated with the same bacteria as is used in Bulgarian yoghurt, which keeps for a few days. Attempts are currently being made to produce a cheese from this camel's milk, even though it appears to be somewhat unsuitable.

For Hindus the cow is a sacred animal. In the Brahmanic ritual its five products – milk, curds, butter, urine and dung – are instruments of purification. Cheese is made from cow's milk, but also from buffalo's milk, this animal being excluded from the veneration accorded the cow, while yielding distinctly more milk. Since maturation poses problems during the hot humid season, smoking is preferred as a means of preservation. The cheese thus takes on a spicy taste, especially when the fire is made from dried cow dung, the usual fuel in unwooded regions and in the Himalayas.

BANDAL is one of these smoked Indian cheeses, found all over the country. The curds are separated using lemon juice and are then shaped and drained in little baskets, before being smoked. The cheese is fine, smooth and highly aromatic. Bandal is usually eaten fresh. DACCA, a pressed, smoked cheese of two months maturation, is a speciality of southern India. SURATI, a buffalo's milk cheese, which has taken the name of the town of Surat near Bombay, is reputed for its nutritional and medicinal qualities. A vegetable rennet is added to the milk (Hindus being vegetarian). The curds mature in their whey and are preserved in large pots. In the southeast, where bubals (of the buffalo family) take the place of cows, buffalo cheese is also made, from soured milk curdled with vegetable rennet. The curds are pressed and soaked in brine.

Ghi (clarified butter), Damir and Pamir; three Indian cheeses (TOP CENTRE). ABOVE: a Nepalese shepherd, near Dilikot. BOTTOM: milking the cattle in the state of Uttarpradesh, in northern India.

NEW WORLDS

settlers arrived. Agriculture developed in those regions where the climate was suitable, namely the south and areas affected by the ocean's influence. For the farmers, selling calves in town was a profitable business, while cow's milk could be made into cheese, which was particularly appreciated in mid-winter, when the milk yield was low and snow covered the land for many long months. By the beginning of the 19th century, cheese manufacture was widespread in Quebec, Ontario and in the coastal regions. By mid-century, these same provinces between them had 500,000 cows. Farmers made cheeses resembling those of their native lands, but through variations in the soil, the climate and the herds, they gradually grew into new types of cheese.

The greatest change happened in 1865 through the agency of Harvey Farrington, a cheese-maker from Oxford County, Ontario. In his modern dairy,

A poster for the "Canadian Mite" of 1892, the largest cheese ever made (TOP). BELOW: a farm in the Simcoë region, Ontario, Canada.

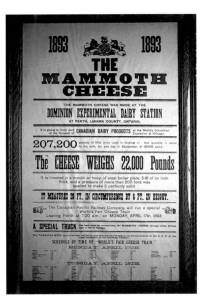

which he did not hesitate to call *The Pioneer*, he experimented with a new English method of making Cheddar cheese, which was an instant hit with traders and consumers. Over the next few years, several hundred dairies took up making Cheddar using this process. Canada made its entry into the world of cheese with a spectacular feat still in the record books today: the production of a giant Cheddar weighing 10 tonnes to mark the 1893 World Exhibition held in Chicago. The cheese was called "The Canadian Mite" and made in Perth, Ontario, using 103,000 litres of milk. It finished up in a London restaurant, where it was cut open using gardening tools. After maturing for 2 years and touring the Old and New Worlds, this fabulous cheese was still delighting the gourmets. Its birthplace basked in

the reflected glory of its fame, with exports of Canadian Cheddar soaring to 234 million lbs of cheese by 1904, although this figure has never since been surpassed. In its efforts to maintain the lead given by this record-breaking cheese, Canada has continued to play the modernisation card. In 1974, milk from a 7-year-old Holstein-Friesian cow, called Ingholm Rag Apple President, broke the record for fat content, with 36,964 litres of milk containing 2098 lbs of fatty matter.

CANADIAN CHEDDAR

Since the famous 1893 Exhibition, Canadian Cheddar has earned its laurels in the international markets. It is made from unskimmed milk and sold at different degrees of maturation: mild, medium or strong. A large proportion of it is used to make cheese spreads. Cheddar is sold in rounds or large rectangular blocks, which may weigh up to 40 kg. The fat content is usually restricted to a maximum of 48%. The Californian variant of Cheddar, MONTEREY JACK, has also been made in Canada since 1970.

■ CANADIAN CHEDDAR

Cow's milk cheese (30 to 50% fat)

TYPE: semi-hard, straw coloured;

firm, natural rind

SHAPE: cylinder or block

WEIGHT: about 15 to 40 kg

RICHELIEU

The aftermath of the Second World War brought a tide of immigrants flooding into Canada. These immigrants did not come alone. With them came the washed cheeses of northern Europe and, above all, Italian cheeses, to be eaten with pasta and spaghetti. Richelieu is in fact Italian Bel Paese cheese. Known in Canada as BUTTER-CHEESE, it was introduced to Henryville in Quebec in 1935. Production of the cheese was subsequently abandoned, but it was resumed again in 1960. It is sold in blocks of under 2 kg.

■ RICHELIEU

Cow's milk cheese (50% fat)

TYPE: soft, white creamy texture; bloomy

SHAPE: rectangular block

WEIGHT: 2 kg

OTHER CHEESES

At the beginning of the century, a version of Belgian Limburger cheese was introduced to Ontario. Production of this soft cheese was resumed in 1964, with a few adjustments in accord with American demand. Another washed cheese, called AMERICAN MUNSTER, made in Canada and exported to the United States, is also worth a mention. RACLETTE, a cheese of Swiss origin, is very fashionable in the ski resorts of this snow-covered land. It has only been made in Canada for the last twenty years or so, but it has been spectacularly successful. The 125,000 kg produced annually in 1989 may well have quadrupled by the early- to mid-1990s. The 1960s also saw the introduction of OKA cheese resembling French Port-Salut, originally made by the monks of

the Trappist Monastery in Quebec from 1881 onwards and later sold commercially. This rubbery-textured cheese has proved popular with the Canadians and production has increased dramatically, reaching almost

175,000 kg a year. The cheese is round-shaped, weighing from 500 g to 2 kg and containing 45% fat. Immigration into Canada since the Second World War has resulted in more than sixty new types of cheese, among them sheep's milk TUMA cheese (of Sicilian origin), TRECCE (an Italian *pasta filata* cheese) and SERRA (from mountain regions of Portugal).

A cattle drive on the Canadian border. Big Beaver, Saskatchewan, Canada (TOP).

BOTTOM LEFT: Richelieu.

LEFT: Oka.

Mitla cathedral,
Mexico (BELOW).
TOP: a Mexican market:
a selection of Oaxaca
cheeses. PRECEDING
PAGES: a sheepfold
in the Cordillera des
Andes, near Salta,
north-west Argentina.

When Portuguese and Spanish navigators set off on their conquest of the high seas, such journeys were a risky business. Their little caravels were the only ships of the period capable of embarking on the discovery of "new stars". Journeys took forever and food was a crucial problem. Procuring supplies of fresh water was already a major feat. Hard sheep's cheeses of the Manchego type were a royal feast for the penniless gentlemen who set sail with a handful of adventurers in the hope of carving out kingdoms for themselves at the ends of the earth. There was no trace of cheese in the lands they found, which could at best offer only the milk of llamas, those strange camel-headed beasts who lived high up on the plateaus of the Andes. This was nothing to the surprise of the indigenous Indians however, when they saw beings straight out of legend disembarking from the ship: men on horseback. The discovery of America brought the world potatoes, maize, tomatoes, cocoa and a multitude of other edible plants which transformed the habits of many peoples and helped to bring their famines under control. For their part, the conquerors brought cattle, sheep and a few goats, and with them, the potential for making cheese. The papal blessing bestowed on these adventurers also extended to the provision of specialist cheese-makers, in the form of the monks who travelled with them. The north-south running *cordilleras* and high plateaus of Latin America, so free of tropical diseases, were gradually turned over to stock-rearing. These unhoped-for animals – a few per family – provided the local populations with milk. The Spanish, Portuguese and later, Italian colonisers replicated the sizeable estates of their native lands, developing non-intensive stock-keeping on the great grassy plains and endless pampas.

The poor peasants and the village communities used the milk to make cheese. Although much less diversified, their cheeses sometimes recalled those of old Europe, particularly those of the Latin countries, whose languages Latin America already shared. The most widespread locally-produced cheese is Queso Blanco, *fromage blanc* or soft white cheese, which is made just about everywhere under various names, either fresh or semi-matured. The production of cheese in Latin American countries is expanding rapidly. Cattle and pasture are indeed plentiful. Yet the dairy industry has tended to concentrate on making European semi-hard cheeses, of the Emmental or Dutch cheese type, already tried and trusted the world over.

Mexico, the largest country in Central America, is notorious for its tumultuous political life and its revolutions. Agricultural reform was undertaken at the beginning of the century, as a result of the revolutionary uprisings of the peasant leaders, Pancho Villa and Zapata. Even though the *peones* possess their own land and herds, the large estates have not actually disappeared, and most livestock is still raised for its meat.

OAXACA or ASADERO is an unskimmed cow's milk cheese. It is by far the most widespread. It is a *pasta filata* cheese, kneaded then formed into a ball-shape which is plunged in brine for several minutes. A cheese may be one of several different shapes, and weighs roughly 250 g to 2 kg. It is straw coloured, contains 45% fat, and comes in a plastic wrapping.

ANEJO is a traditional skimmed goat's milk cheese (sometimes cow's milk). It is a soft cheese weighing about 5 kg and sold in canvas pouches. GAJAQUENO is another goat's cheese of the *pasta filata* variety. In the south of the country, particularly along the coast, the vegetation has a tropical character. COYOLITO, a semi-hard cheese washed in coconut milk, is made there. It is matured for 3 months, with regular salt water washes, and has a slightly pungent flavour. There are also a number of very hard, salty cheeses, matured for a year or more and related to Parmesan.

Soft white cheese, or QUESO BLANCO, is very popular with the Andean peasants, who make it under local names. Cheeses are for the most part little matured, since the people are not too keen on the pungent taste of more matured cheeses. Between the very high altitude pastures with their short grass, and the steamy and overheated lowlands, there is not much room for rearing cattle in acceptable conditions. The Andean

countries produce a number of cheeses but their characteristics are ill-defined. Nonetheless, several *pasta filata* type cheeses can be identified in Colombia, among them PERA, which is made from skimmed cow's milk, and sold in tiny morsels, after a very short maturation. The situation is very different in Argentina, where the exportation of meat fired a major boom in the period between the wars. The arrival of Italian immigrants enriched the local production of soft cheeses, leading to cheeses such as CHUBUT, CUARTIROLO, GOYA, which is essentially a little-

matured Asiago, and MOLITERNO a *pasta filata* cheese. Parmesan, essential for giving soul to spaghetti and tagliatelli dishes, finds its local equivalent in TREBOLGIANO. TREBOLGIANO CHICO is matured for 12 months, while TREBOLGIANO GRANDE takes 18 months. Like Argentina, Brazil is a major stockbreeding country, but most animals are destined for the butcher's knife. However, in the state of Minas Gerais, they make a cheese called MINAS FRESCAL, a soft cheese made from the milk of Suri cattle. MINAS PRENSADO is another soft cheese, made by heating the curds, then straining and kneading them, before pressing them into a mould.

Drying goat cheeses in Huanuco, Peru (BOTTOM LEFT). The drying is accelerated by lighting a fire beneath the cheeses. CENTRE: San José market, Costa Rica. TOP: Aymara Indian women selling their cheeses at market, Bolivia. BELOW: Angora goats and sheep in Argentina.

Melbourne harbour in the province of Victoria, southern Australia (BOTTOM). Drawing by E de Bérard, based on a photograph (1861). TOP: sheep farming in Australia. Sheep are raised for their wool, meat and, of course, their milk.

Although it was discovered in 1606 (Tasmania remained unknown until 1643), and visited on a number of subsequent occasions, Australia was not peopled by Europeans until 1788. Then it was that the English set up the Botany Bay penal colony in New South Wales, no doubt filling it with quite as many poor innocent wretches as actual criminals. The few horses and sheep, and the half-dozen cattle who accompanied the first exiles, were intended to provide food for the governors of this antipodean prison, rather than to enhance the lives of its inmates. Settlers did not start to come of their own free will until much later, although by 1830, they outnumbered the convicts. It was not until the end of the 19th century, with the exploration of the interior and the north of the country, that the Europeans finally realised that this vast island – or rather continent – had been inhabited for thousands of years by an aboriginal population, unaware of either agriculture or metals. The first cattle introduced to the country were mostly reared for meat; cow's milk was used only for the domestic needs of the breeders. By the mid-19th century however, good Jersey dairy cattle were thick on the ground. Cheddar cheese soon followed, as part of a current policy of introducing the cheese to all those corners of the British Empire where conditions were suitable. This traditional English cheese was made by a new process which enabled it to be manufactured in large quantities, a revolutionary development which took cheese-making straight from a cottage industry into the industrial era. From then on, Australia began to produce cheese or, more precisely, and almost exclusively, Cheddar, making the most of the lush green pastures of Queensland, New South Wales and later, Tasmania.

At the end of the last war, at which point 90% of the population was of British or Irish origin, Australia opened its doors to immigration. Italians, Greeks, Maltese, Dutch, Polish and Turks arrived in large numbers. Many of them brought their own customs, cuisine and cheeses with them. Through the pizzerias that they opened, the Italians introduced soft, elastic-textured *pasta filata* cheeses, reminiscent of Caciocavallo. Thus, MOZZARELLA, PROVOLONE and SCARMOZE, a gourd-shaped cheese, matured for only one month, are all produced in Australia. An impressive array of Italian hard cheeses can also be found, including PARMESAN, made with the milk of the many sheep in Australia (which yield more than just wool), ROMANO, PECORINO, PEPATO – seasoned with grains of pepper – and RIGATINO.

246

In 1984, the national production of Australian blue cheese, GIPPSLAND BLUE (named after the richest milk-producing area of the continent situated in the south-east) amounted to 6 tonnes. Since then, this cheese has become a sort of legend in Australia and several hundred tonnes are now produced a year. One of the main architects of its success is Richard Thomas, who went to seek out the secrets of production directly from the makers of Novara Gorgonzola. There is also EDAM (matured for 2 to 6 months), GOUDA (matured for 3 to 6 months), and various types of GRUYÈRE and EMMENTAL, such as SAMSØ and TILSIT, which are used for fondue and sandwiches. Australian Kefalotyri (of Greek origin), is called KEFALOGRAVIERA. HALOUMY is a cheese seasoned with herbs and matured in its whey. A pale yellow cow's milk version of FETA cheese is also available, made, like Haloumy, from skimmed milk. Both cheeses are very popular with the Australians because of their low fat content. Bloomy cheeses are present in the form of BRIE and CAMEMBERT.

AUSTRALIAN CHEDDAR

Over half the cheese produced in Australia is either Cheddar or Cheshire

(70,000 tonnes in 1989). There are several varieties of Cheddar however. The most popular with lovers of cheese is undoubtedly Farmhouse Cheddar, sold at 4 different stages of maturation. "Mild", which has a fine, delicate flavour, is matured for 3 months. The richly flavoured "Semi-Mature" is matured for less than 6 months. "Mature" Cheddar takes up to 1 year to mature, bringing out all the qualities of this great cheese. "Vintage" Cheddar, aimed at the most pernickety connoisseurs, is a rich yellow colour and tastes a little pungent. It is matured for up to 18 months. The production methods of pasteurised Cheddar are practically identical in every large dairy the world over. Australian dairies tend to have the most up to date amenities however. In one cooperative dairy in Bega (New South Wales) for example, whose plant is only 20 years old, the pasteurised milk is processed in 14,000-litre vats. The curds are produced at

a temperature of 31° C by the addition of rennet and lactic acid. They are then broken up into small pieces. These fragments are slowly heated to 38° C with the whey for 40 minutes and then kneaded so that the curds harden and the whey is strained off. After 2 to 3 hours of this, the curds and whey are pumped out of the vat.

The curds are tipped into the moulds and left to stand for 2 hours until they set to the firmness required. Next they undergo the process known as "cheddaring". As soon as the desired level of acidity is attained, the whey is drained out of the vat. The curds are beaten against the sides of the vat to make this easier. The true "cheddaring" now begins. The curds are cut into long thick slices, then beaten several times (moving the curds at the bottom up to the top each time). When the acidity level is right, the curds are broken into 2-centimetre cubes. 2.5% salt is added

"Vintage" Cheddar (ABOVE). TOP: "Mature" Cheddar. BELOW: cattle and cockatoos in Queensland, Australia.

and the curds are kneaded to ensure that the salt is evenly spread. The curds are then placed into hoops to be pressed overnight. The next day, the block of Cheddar is cut up into smaller blocks, which are wrapped in a plastic film, which must be tight-fitting to prevent any air from getting in. These are then put to mature. Making Cheddar with pasteurised milk rather weakens its original flavour, so it is often pepped up with garlic, onion, chives, aromatic herbs, pepper, paprika or bacon and sometimes even wine, added during its maturation. There is also a smoked variety of Cheddar, made by placing the cheese in a smoky environment for 6 hours.

■ AUSTRALIAN CHEDDAR

Pasteurised cow's milk (50% fat)

TYPE: semi-hard, orange to white coloured; dry rind

SHAPE: cylinder or rectangular block

WEIGHT: cylinders, 5, 10 and 20 kg; blocks, 250 and 500 g

PRESENTATION: in plastic wrapper

OTHER CHEESES

No cheese-making industry, however up to date, can hope to flourish without the inspirational presence and flavours of farm-produced cheeses. For the past 20 years therefore, farmers have been making cheeses not just for their own use but for sale in specialised shops. Only they can really give their farm-made cheeses the taste of the earth so appreciated by gourmets and so lacking in industrially-made cheeses, whose flavours never vary. Camembert, Brie, Gruyère, Emmental, Montasio and Cabécou-style goat's cheeses are all made in this way in Victoria and, in particular, in Tasmania.

New Zealand was not born when the Dutch sailor, Abel Janszoon Tasman discovered it in 1642, or even when James Cook, the famous Captain who gave his name to the straits separating the two main islands, set foot there. Its first inhabitants were the Maoris, who came to this fertile promised land from Polynesia in the 1st century AD. Like all Pacific peoples however, they knew nothing of cattle, goats or sheep before the English arrived there, first as explorers, and, from 1838 onwards, as settlers. Cheese was already being exported from New Zealand by 1846 and, as for many other territories under the British Crown, cheese production really took off there in the mid-19th century. The discovery of gold seams in the 1870s led to a major influx of immigrants. In the course of this decade, the European population increased from 100,000 to 256,000. A few Jersey cows, chosen for

Thirsty livestock approaching the water (BOTTOM). Queensland, Australia. TOP: a New Zealand shepherd keeping watch over his immense flock, from horseback.

their high milk yield, were brought over from England to try their luck on the vast pastures of the antipodes. With them came the recipe for making Cheddar. The first industrial dairy worthy of the name was opened as a cooperative near Dunedin in 1871. Success came quickly and, half a century later, 510 such dairies were up and running. In the meantime, New Zealand had started to export cheese to England, helped by the use of boxes made of strips of wood, similar to those contributing to the rise of French Camembert in the same period. It was in fact wood's capacity to absorb any surplus moisture which made it possible to send the cheeses overseas to the other side of the world. Before the end of the 19th century however, refrigerator ships had offered a more modern solution to the problem of transportation.

NEW ZEALAND CHEDDAR

A new wave of immigration, after the last war, brought in its wake a marked nostalgia for the traditions of the old countries. Industrialists and artisans fell to making Italian, Greek, Dutch and Danish cheeses, thus diversifying the indigenous dairy industry. New Zealand currently produces over 50 cheeses which are variants on great European names, but Cheddar still rules supreme. Its four basic forms are all made: Mild, Semi-Matured, Mature and Vintage, their character always remaining consistent.

■ NEW ZEALAND CHEDDAR

Skimmed cow's milk cheese

(35 to 45% fat)

TYPE: pressed, semi-hard; rindless

SHAPE: wedge

WEIGHT: 250 g to 1 kg, up to 1.9 kg for Vintage

MATURATION: Mild, 6 months; Tasty, 6 to 12 months; Vintage 18 to 24 months

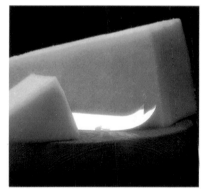

OTHER CHEESES

COLBY has a softer, more rubbery texture than Cheddar, and is pocked with minute holes. It is not a "cheddarised" cheese. Slices of Colby are popular as an accompaniment to salads. It is very widely sold in the United States, destination of many of New Zealand's exported dairy products. It is sold

in blocks weighing 250 g to 1 kg. KAHURANGI is a "Brie-style Blue" smooth, creamy and slightly acidic. It has a mousse-like consistency when ripe. KIKURANGI, a "firm blue cheese" is golden coloured, rich and buttery, with a creamy flavour. TUPIHI is a typical New Zealand cheese, whose name comes from the Maori word for thin and without fat. Its medium flavour strengthens with age. It is used as a Cheddar substitute. Coated in a layer of red paraffin, it is, as its name suggests, a low-fat cheese. The entire range of classic cheeses -EDAM, FETA, MOZZARELLA (made with cow's milk), PYRENEES and so on – is made in reduced-fat varieties. COTTAGE CHEESE, RICOTTA and QUARK are the classic low-fat cheeses made here.

Kahurangi (TOP). CENTRE: New Zealand Cheddar. BELOW: view across the Coromandel peninsula along the northern coast of New Zealand.

TABLE OF CHEESES

While this list includes all those cheeses mentioned in the present work, and many more besides, it cannot, of course, claim to be exhaustive. Cheeses are listed by country or region of origin. The type of milk usually used to make them is also indicated.

AFGHANISTAN, IRAN
Kadchgall – sheep/camel
Serat – sheep

ALGERIA, MOROCCO, TUNISIA
Sardo – sheep
Sicile – sheep
Testouri – sheep/goat

ARGENTINA
Chubut – cow
Cuartirolo – cow
Goya – cow
Moliterno – cow
Pepato – cow
Queso Blanco – cow
Tandil – cow
Trebolgiano – cow

AUSTRALIA
Australian Cheddar – cow
Australian Parmesan – sheep
Gippsland Blue – cow
Haloumy – cow/sheep
Kefalograviera – sheep
Maczola – cow
Pepato – cow
Rigatino – cow
Scarmorze – cow

AUSTRIA
Bergkäse – cow
Dule – cow
Gussing – cow
Hauerkäse – cow
Imperial Frischkäse – cow
Jochberg – cow/goat
Kugelkäse – cow
Luneberg – cow
Marienhofer – cow
Mischling – cow
Mondseer Schachtelkäse – cow
Montavoner – cow
Olmutzer Bierkäse – cow
Pinzgauer Bierkäse – cow
Prälatenkäse – cow
Quargel (aka Sauerkäse) – cow
Rahmkäse – cow
Salami – cow
Schwarzenberger – cow
Schloss – cow
Tanzenberger – cow
Trappistenkäse – cow
Tyroler Alpkäse – cow
Tyroler Graukäse – cow

BALKANS
Bracki Sir – sheep
Kajmak – sheep
Licki – sheep
Manur – cow/sheep
Mrsav – sheep
Pagó – sheep
Paski Sir – cow
Pirotski Katschkawalj – sheep
Posni Sir – sheep
Presukaca – sheep
Quacheq – sheep
Silba – cow
Sir Mastni – sheep
Siraz – cow
Siriz Mjesine – sheep
Tord – sheep
Travnik – sheep
Tvdr Sir – sheep
Vlasic – sheep
Zlatiborski – sheep

BALTIC
Sovietski – cow
Latviiski – cow

BELGIUM
Aettekees (aka Brusselskaas) – cow
Beauvoorde – cow
Bierkäse – cow
Broodkaas – cow
Cassette – cow
Castellum – cow
Chimay – cow
Herve – cow
Hette-kees (aka Stink-kees) – cow
Macquée – cow
Maredsous – cow
Orval – cow
Passendale – cow
Plateau – cow
Plattekees – cow
Pottekees – cow
Remoudou – cow
Royal Brabant – cow
Rubens – cow

BRAZIL
Coalhada – cow
Minas Frescal – cow
Minas Prensado – cow
Prato – cow
Queso Blanco – cow
Requeijão – cow

BULGARIA
Katschkawalj – sheep
Sirene – sheep/cow
Siriz – sheep
Teleme – sheep/goat
Yoghurt – cow/sheep/ goat/buffalo

CANADA
American Munster – cow
Canadian Cheddar – cow
Monterey Jack – cow
Oka – cow
Raclette – cow
Richelieu (aka Butter Cheese) – cow
Serra – sheep
Trecce – cow
Tuma – sheep

CAUCASUS
Altaiski – cow
Brynza – cow/sheep
Daralagjazky – sheep/cow
Erevanski – cow/sheep
Gorny – cow/sheep
Gornyaltajski – sheep
Kefir – cow/sheep/goat
Kobiiski – cow/sheep
Lescin – sheep
Motal – cow/sheep
Msitra – sheep
Ossetin – cow/sheep
Soulougouni – cow
Tchanakh – cow
Telpanir – sheep/cow
Touchinski – cow/sheep
Travnik – sheep

COLOMBIA
Pera – cow
Queso Blanco – cow
Queso Estera – cow

CRETE
Graviera – cow
Kritiko – sheep
Mitzithra – goat/sheep

CYPRUS
Anari – sheep/goat
Halloumi – sheep/goat
Kaskavali – sheep

CZECH AND SLOVAK STATES
Abertam – sheep
Bryndza – sheep
Koppen – goat
Olmutzer Quargel – sheep/ cow
Oschtjepka – sheep
Parenica – sheep
Riesengebirge – goat

DENMARK
Appetitost – cow
Danablu (aka Danish Blue, Marmora) – cow
Danbo – cow
Danish Export – cow
Elbo – cow
Esrom (aka Danish Port-Salut) – cow
Fynbo – cow
Gislev – cow
Havarti – cow
Kjarsgaard – cow
Kuminost – cow
Maribo – cow
Molbo – cow
Mycella – cow
Runesten – cow
Samsø – cow
Svenbo – cow
Tybo – cow
Tykmaelk – cow

EGYPT
Beda – sheep
Domiati – cow
Kareish – cow
Misch – goat/sheep
Rumi – cow/goat

EUROPEAN RUSSIA
Chletsarski – cow
Daralagjazsky – cow
Gorny – cow
Kostromskoi – cow
Moskovski – cow
Stepnoi – cow

FINLAND
Aura – cow
Ilves – reindeer
Juhla – cow
Juustoleipa – cow
Kartano – cow
Korsholm – cow
Kreim – cow
Munajuusto – cow
Tutunmaa – cow

FRANCE
Abondance – cow
Ami de Chambertin – cow
Anost – cow
Ardéchois – goat
Ardi-Gasna (aka Arnéguy) – sheep
Arthon – goat
Asco – sheep/goat
Aunis – cow/goat
Autun – cow/goat
Baguette Laonnaise – cow
Banon – cow/sheep
Banon au Poivre d'Ane – goat/cow
Beauceron – goat
Beaufort – cow
Bessay en Chaume – goat
Bethmale – cow/goat/ sheep
Béthune – cow
Bleu d'Auvergne – cow
Bleu de Bresse – cow
Bleu des Causses – cow
Bleu de Cayres – cow
Bleu de Corse – sheep
Bleu de Gex (aka Bleu de Septmoncel) – cow
Bleu du Haut-Jura – cow
Bleu de Laqueuille – cow

Bleu de Lavaldens – cow

Bleu de Loudes – cow

Bleu du Quercy – cow

Bleu du Queyras – cow

Bleu de Sassenage – cow

Bleu de Thiézac – cow

Bleu de Velay – cow

Bondart (aka Bondon) –
   cow

Bougon – goat

Bouille – cow

Boulette d'Avesnes – cow

Boursault – cow

Bouton-de-Culotte – goat

Bressan (aka Thoissey) –
   cow/goat

Bricquebec – cow

Brie – cow

Brie de Coulommiers – cow

Brie de Macquelines – cow

Brie de Meaux – cow

Brie de Melun – cow

Brie de Melun Bleu – cow

Brie de Montereau – cow

Brie de Nangis – cow

Brillat-Savarin – cow

Brin d'Amour (aka Fleur du
   Maquis) – goat

Brique du Forez – goat

Brique du Livradois – goat

Broccio (aka Brucciu) –
   goat

Brousse – sheep

Bûche Forézienne – cow

Bûchette d'Anjou – goat

Cabécou – goat

Cabrion – goat

Cachat – goat/sheep

Cahors – goat

Cailloux du Rhône – cow

Cajassous – goat

Calenzana – goat

Camembert – cow

Cancoillotte – cow

Cantal – cow

Carré de Bray – cow

Carré de l'Est – cow

Cendré d'Argonne – cow

Cendré de Champagne –
   cow

Cendré de Rocroi – cow

Chabichou – goat

Chabricon – goat

Chabris – goat

Chambérat – cow

Chanteloup – goat

Chaource – cow

Charolles – goat/cow

Chasteau – cow

Chaunay – goat

Chauny – cow

Chevrotin des Aravis – goat

Chevrotin du Bourbonnais –
   goat

Chevroton – goat

Chouzé – goat

Cierp – cow

Cîteaux – cow

Civray – goat

Claquebitou – goat

Claqueret – cow

Comté – cow

Coulommiers – cow

Creusois – cow

Crézancy – goat

Croix d'Or – goat

Crottin de Chavignol – goat

Cubjac – goat

Dauphin (Dauphiné) – cow

Dornecy – goat

Dreux à la Feuille – cow

Echourgnac – cow

Emmental – cow

Entrammes – cow

Entraygue – goat/sheep

Epoisses – cow

Ercé – cow

Esbareich – sheep

Excelsior – cow

Fontal – cow

Fougeru – cow

Fourme d'Ambert – cow

Fourme de Montbrizon –
   cow

Gaperon – cow

Gardian – sheep

Gautrias – cow

Gauville – cow

Géromé (aka Munster des
   Vosges) – cow

Gevrey – goat

Gien – goat/cow

Golo – sheep

Gournay – cow

Graçay – goat

Gras des Bauges – cow

Gris de Lille (aka Gros
   Puant, etc.) – cow

Gruyère des Bauges – cow

Guerbigny – cow

Guéret – cow

Gueyin – cow

Hauteluce – goat

Heiltz-le-Maurupt – cow

Igny – cow

Joux (Vacherin de) – cow

Jumeaux – goat

Laguiole – cow

Langres – cow

Laruns – sheep

Laval – cow

Levroux – goat

Ligueil – goat

Liniez – goat

Lisieux – cow

Livarot – cow

Livernon – goat

Livron – goat

Lormes – cow

Lucullus – cow

Lusignan – goat

Macquelines – cow

Mamirolle – cow

Maroilles – cow

Mignon – cow

Mignot Blanc – cow

Mimolette – cow

Mont-Cenis – cow/goat

Mont des Cats – cow

Mont-Dore – cow

Montfort – cow

Montoire – goat

Morbier – cow

Mothais – goat

Mothe-Saint-Héray – goat

Moulins – goat

Munster – cow

Muntanacciu – sheep

Mur de Barez – goat

Murol – cow

Neufchâtel – cow

Nioio – goat/sheep

Oléron – sheep

Olivet – cow

Oloron – sheep

Orrys – sheep/cow

Ossau-Iraty – sheep

Oust – cow

Oustet – cow

Parthenay – goat

Pavé Blésois – goat

Pavé d'Auge – cow

Pavé de Moyaux – cow

Pavé de Valençay – goat

Pavin – cow

Pélardon – goat

Pelvoux – cow

Pérail – sheep

Persillé des Aravis – goat

Persillé du Mont-Cenis –
   cow

Petit Lisieux – cow

Petit-Suisse – cow

Petit Tnoly – cow

Picodon – goat

Pierre-qui-Vire – cow

Pithiviers – cow

Pont-l'Evêque – cow

Port-Salut – cow

Pougny – goat

Pouligny-St-Pierre – goat

Puant Macéré – cow

Reblochon – cow

Ribot – cow

Riceys (Les) – cow

Ricotta aux Galets – goat

Rigotte de Condrieu –cow/
   goat

Rocamadour – sheep

Rochefort – cow

Rocroi – cow

Rollot – cow

Roncal – cow

Roquefort – sheep

Ruffec – goat

Saint-Afrique – goat

Saint-Fargeol – cow

Saint-Florentin – cow

Saint-Gildas – cow

Saint-Lizier – cow

Saint-Loup sur-Thouet –
   goat

Saint-Marcellin – cow/goat

Saint-Nectaire – cow

Saint-Paulin – cow

Saint-Saulge – goat

Sainte-Anne-d'Auray –
   cow

Sainte-Marie – goat/cow

Sainte-Maure – goat

Salers Haute Montagne –
   cow

Sancerre – goat

Santranges – goat

Sartenais – sheep/goat

Sarténo-Fumé – sheep/goat

Selles-sur-Cher – goat

Semussac – cow

Sérac – cow

Sollies-Toucas – goat

Sorbais – cow

Sospel – cow

Tamié – cow

Tarare – cow

Tardets – cow

Tignard – cow/goat

Tomme au Marc – cow

Tomme d'Abondance –
   cow

Tomme d'Annot – goat

Tomme de Belley – cow

Tomme de Brach – sheep

Tomme de Champsaur –
   goat

Tomme de Combovin –
   goat

Tomme de Corps – goat

Tomme de Crest – goat

Tomme de Praslin – goat

Tomme de Queyras – goat

Tomme de Romans – cow

Tomme de Saint-Marcellin
   – cow

Tomme de Savoie – cow

Tomme des Allues – cow

Tomme des Aravis – cow

Tomme du Revard – goat

Tomme du Vivarais – goat/
   cow

Toucy – goat

Toupin – cow

Tracy – goat

Trappiste – cow

Trou du Murol – cow

Troyes (Troyen) – cow

Urt – cow

Vacherin d'Abondance –
   cow

Vacherin des Bauges –
   cow

Valençay – goat

Varennes – goat

Venaco – goat/sheep

Vendôme Bleu – cow

Vendôme Cendré – cow

Vermenton – goat

Vézelay – goat

Vic-en-Bigorre – sheep

Villebarou – cow

Xaintray – goat

TABLE OF CHEESES

GERMANY

Allgäuer Emmentaler – cow
Allgäuer Limburger – cow
Altenburger-Milbenkäse – cow
Altenburger – goat
Bavarian Bergkäse – cow
Bayernland – cow
Bergader – cow
Bierkäse – cow
Brioler – cow
Bruder Basil – cow
Butterkäse – cow
Dreizeitige – cow
Edelpilzkäse (aka Pitzkäse) – cow
Frühstück – cow
Gaiskäsli – goat
Geheimratskäse – cow
Handkäse – cow
Harzkäse – cow
Herbst – cow
Ihlefeld – cow
Limburger – cow
Mainzerkäse – cow
Mecklenburg – cow
Montagnolo – cow
Montsalvat – cow
Münster – cow
Nieheimer Hopfen – cow
Quark – cow
Radener – cow
Ragnit – cow
Rahm – cow
Raucherkäse – cow
Rinnen – cow
Romadur – cow
Schloss – cow
Schmelkäse – cow
Schnittkäse – cow
Spitz – cow
Stangen – cow
Steinbuscher – cow
Süssmilch – cow
Thuringia – cow
Tilsit – cow
Topfen – cow
Trappist – cow
Wasserburger – cow
Weisslacker – cow
Werder – cow
Wilstermarsch – cow
Woriener – cow
Ziegenkäse – goat
Zweitzeitige – cow

GREAT BRITAIN

Beenleigh Blue – sheep
Berkeley – cow
Blue Cheshire – cow
Blue Wensleydale – cow
Bonchester – cow
Brickbat – cow
Caboc – cow
Caerphilly – cow
Cambridge – cow
Cardigan – cow
Charnwood – cow
Cheddar – cow
Cheshire – cow
Colby – cow
Coon – cow
Cotherstone – cow
Cotswold – cow
Cottenham – cow
Cottage Cheese – cow
Crowdie – cow
Cumberland Farmhouse – cow
Daventry – cow
Derby – cow
Devonshire – cow
Dorset Blue Vinney – cow
Double Gloucester – cow
Dunlop – cow
Dunsyre Blue – cow
Essex – cow
Islay – cow
Lanark Blue – sheep
Lancashire – cow
Leicester – cow
Lincoln – cow
Llanboidy – cow
Llangloffan – cow
Marianglas – goat
Nessel – cow
Norfolk – cow
Orkney – cow
Pant-y-Llyn – cow
Pencarreg – cow
Sage Derby – cow
Sherwood – cow
Shropshire Blue – cow
Single Gloucester – cow
Slipcote – cow
Staffordshire – cow
Stilton – cow
Suffolk – cow
Swaledale – cow
Truckles – cow
Tynlgrug – cow
Walton – cow
Warwickshire – cow
Wedmore – cow
Wensleydale – cow
White Wensleydale – cow
Wiltshire – cow
Windsor – cow
Yarg – cow
York – cow

GREAT PLAINS

Dessertnyj Belyj – cow
Karpatski – cow
Kubanski – cow
Lioubitelski – cow
Pikhantnyj – cow
Voljski – cow
Vologodski – cow
Zakussotchny – cow

GREECE

Anfissis – cow
Feta – sheep/cow/goat
Galotyri – sheep/goat
Kasseri – sheep/goat
Kefalotyri – goat/sheep
Kopanisti – sheep/cow/goat
Manouri – goat/sheep
Salamana – sheep
Skyros – goat/sheep
Touloumisio – cow

HOLLAND

Boeren Liedenkaas – cow
Boerenkaas – cow
Commissiekaas (aka Dutch Mimolette) – cow
Delft – cow
Edam – cow
Fricotal – cow
Friesan Clove (aka Nagelkaas) – cow
Friesekaas (aka Frisian Cheese) – cow
Frison – cow
Gouda – cow
Gouwetaler – cow
Kanterkaas – cow
Kruidkaas – cow
Leerdamer – cow
Leidenkaas – cow
Leidsekaas – cow
Maasdam – cow
Meshanger – cow
Nagelkaas (aka Nageles) – cow
Natte Rabbinale – cow
Texel – sheep
Westberg – cow
West Friesian – cow

HUNGARY

Brynza – sheep
Damen – cow
Harracher – cow
Hochstrasser – cow
Kashkaval – sheep
Kremstaler – cow
Kummel – cow
Kvargli – cow
Liptauer-Brynza (aka Liptoi) – sheep
Ovari – cow
Pannonia – cow
Schwarzenberger – cow

ICELAND

Avaxtskyr – cow
Braudostur – cow
Buri – cow
Dala-Brie – cow
Mysa – cow
Mysingur – cow
Mysuostur – cow
Odalostur – cow
Rjomaskyr – cow
Skyr – cow

INDIA, CENTRAL ASIA

Bandal – cow
Chhana – cow
Dacca – cow
Damir – cow
Karut – cow
Kumiss – horse
Pamir – cow
Surati – buffalo
Withania – cow

IRAQ

Biza – sheep
Fajy – sheep
Jupneh – sheep/goat/camel
Lour – sheep
Meira – sheep
Roos – sheep

IRELAND

Ballydague – cow
Baylough – cow
Blarney – cow
Cashel Blue – cow
Chetwynd Blue – cow
Cooleeney – cow
Corleggy – goat
Cratloe – sheep
Croghan – goat
Desmond – cow
Faiscre Grotha – cow
Gabriel – cow
Grus – cow
Gubbeen – cow
Kerry – cow
Knockanour – cow
Lough Caum – goat
Milleens – cow
Millsen – cow
Mulchan – cow
Ring – cow
Ryefield – cow
Tanag – cow
Tath – cow
Wexford – cow

ISRAEL

Lebbene – sheep/goat
Gwina Zfatit – sheep

ITALY

Asiago d'Allevo – cow
Asiago Pressato – cow
Bagozzo – cow
Bel Paese – cow
Bernade – cow/goat
Bresciano – cow
Cacio Flore – sheep
Caciocavallo – cow
Caciotte – cow
Calcagno – sheep
Canestrato – cow
Caprino – goat
Casigiolc – cow
Castelmagno – cow
Cotronese – sheep
Crescenza – cow
Dolcelatte – cow
Emiliano – cow
Fiore Sardo (Pecorino

252

Sardo) – sheep
Foggiano – sheep
Fontal – cow
Fontina – cow
Fresa – cow
Gorgonzola – cow
Gorgonzola con
   Mascarpone – cow
Grana Padano – cow
Incanestrato – sheep/cow
Majocchino – cow/sheep/goat
Marches – sheep
Mascarpone – cow
Moliterno – cow
Moncenisio – cow
Montasio – cow/goat
Mozzarella – cow/buffalo
Nostrale – cow
Olenda – cow
Panarone – cow
Parmesan (aka Parmigiano
   Reggiano) – cow
Pecorino Romano – sheep
Pecorino Siciliano – sheep
Pressato – cow
Provatura – cow/buffalo
Provole – buffalo
Provolone – cow
Ragusano – cow
Raviggiolo – sheep
Ricotta – cow/sheep
Ricotta Romana – sheep
Riola – goat
Robbiola – cow
Robbiolini – cow/goat/sheep
Romanello – cow
Romano – cow/goat/sheep
Sardo – cow/sheep
Scarmorze – cow
Siago – cow
Siciliano – sheep
Stracchino – cow
Taleggio – cow

Trecce – cow
Vacchino Romano – cow
Veneto – cow

JORDAN
Labaneh – sheep/goat/cow/camel

LEBANON
Akawi – sheep
Chuncliche – sheep/goat
Halloumi – sheep

MAURITANIA
Zrig – goat/camel

MEXICO
Anejo – goat
Asadero (aka Oaxaca) – cow
Coyolito – goat
Gajaqueno – goat
Panela – cow
Queso Anejo – cow/goat

NEW ZEALAND
Colby – cow
Cottage Cheese – cow
Kahurangi – cow
Kikurangi – cow
New Zealand Cheddar – cow
Quark – cow/sheep
Tupihi – cow/sheep

NORWAY
Flötost – cow
Gammelost – cow/goat
Gjetost – cow
Gomost – cow
Jarlsberg – cow
Mysost – cow
Nökkelost – cow
Norbo – cow
Pultost (aka Knaost) – cow

Taffelost – cow
Trönder – cow

POLAND
Olsztynski – cow
Podhalanski – cow/sheep
Trapistaw – cow
Twarogowy – cow/sheep
Tylzscki – cow

PORTUGAL
Alcobaça – sheep
Alentejo – sheep/cow
Alverca – sheep/goat
Alverde – sheep
Azeitão – sheep
Castelo Branco – sheep
Evora – goat/sheep
Ilha do Pico – cow
Ilha São Jorge – cow
Niza – sheep/goat
Rabacal – goat/sheep
Saloio – sheep/cow
Serpa – sheep
Serra – sheep
Thus – sheep
Tomar – sheep

ROMANIA
Brinza – sheep
Burduf – sheep/goat
Cochuletz Brinza – sheep
Halloumi – cow
Monostorer – sheep
Urda – cow/sheep

SPAIN
Alhama – sheep
Aracena – sheep
Armada – sheep
Burgos – sheep
Cabrales – goat
Caciz – sheep
Calahora – sheep
Cantabria – cow

Casteileno – sheep
Cincho – sheep
Conejero – goat
Entzia – sheep
Flor de Guia – sheep/cow
Gorbea – sheep
Hecho – sheep
Idiazabal – sheep
Liebana Picon – sheep/cow/goat
Mahon – cow/sheep
Majorero – goat
Mallorquin – cow/sheep
Manchego – sheep
Nucia – sheep
Orduna – sheep
Perilla – cow
Quesucos – cow/sheep/goat
Roncal – sheep
San Simón – cow
Servilleta – sheep
Tenerife – cow
Ulloa – cow
Urbia – sheep
Villalon – sheep
Zamorano – sheep

SWEDEN
Adelost – cow
Ambrosia – cow
Bondost – cow
Drabant – cow
Gesost – cow
Getmesost – cow
Gotaost (aka Gotland
   Cheese) – goat/cow
Gräddost – cow
Greve – cow
Herrgårdost – cow
Hushållsost – cow
Kryddost – cow
Lapparnas Renost –
   reindeer
Mesost – cow

Prästost – cow
Riddarost – cow
Saarland Pfarr – cow
Sveciaost – cow
Taffelost – cow
Västerbotten – cow
Västgötaost – cow

SWITZERLAND
Alpkäse – cow
Anniviers – cow
Appenzeller – cow
Battelmatt – cow
Bellelay – cow
Chaschol – cow
Christalinna – cow
Conches – cow
Emmental – cow
Fribourg-Vacherin – cow
Gomser – cow
Gruyère – cow
Illiez – cow
Jura – cow
Magerer Schweizerkäse –
   cow
Mainauer – cow
Nidwald – cow
Orsières – cow
Paglia – cow
Piora – cow
Prattigau – cow
Raclette – cow
Rasskäse – cow
Rayon – cow
Rheinwald (aka Schamser) –
   cow
Royalp-Tilsit – cow
Saanen – cow
Sapsago – cow
Sbrinz – cow
Schabzieger – cow
Tête de Moine – cow
Tomme Vaudoise – cow
Uri – cow
Urseren – cow

Vacherin Mont d'Or – cow
Walliser – cow

SYRIA
Lebney – sheep/goat/
   camel

TIBET
Tibet – yak

TURKEY
Beyaz – sheep
Kasar – sheep
Lor – sheep
Mihalic – sheep
Omma – sheep
Salamvra – goat
Tulum – goat

UNITED STATES
American Cheddar – cow
Barrel Cheese – cow
Brick Cheese – cow
Cabot – cow
Colby – cow
Colby Jack – cow
Cottage Cheese – cow
Craigston Camembert – cow
Grafton Village – cow
Great Lakes Cheshire – cow
Kanongan – sheep
Liederkranz – cow
Mammoth Cheese – cow
Monterey Jack – cow
Mountain Shepherd –
   sheep
Serra – goat
Shelburon – cow
Teleme – cow

VENEZUELA
Cuajada – cow
Queso Fresco – cow
Queso de Cavallo – cow
Queso de Cabra – cow

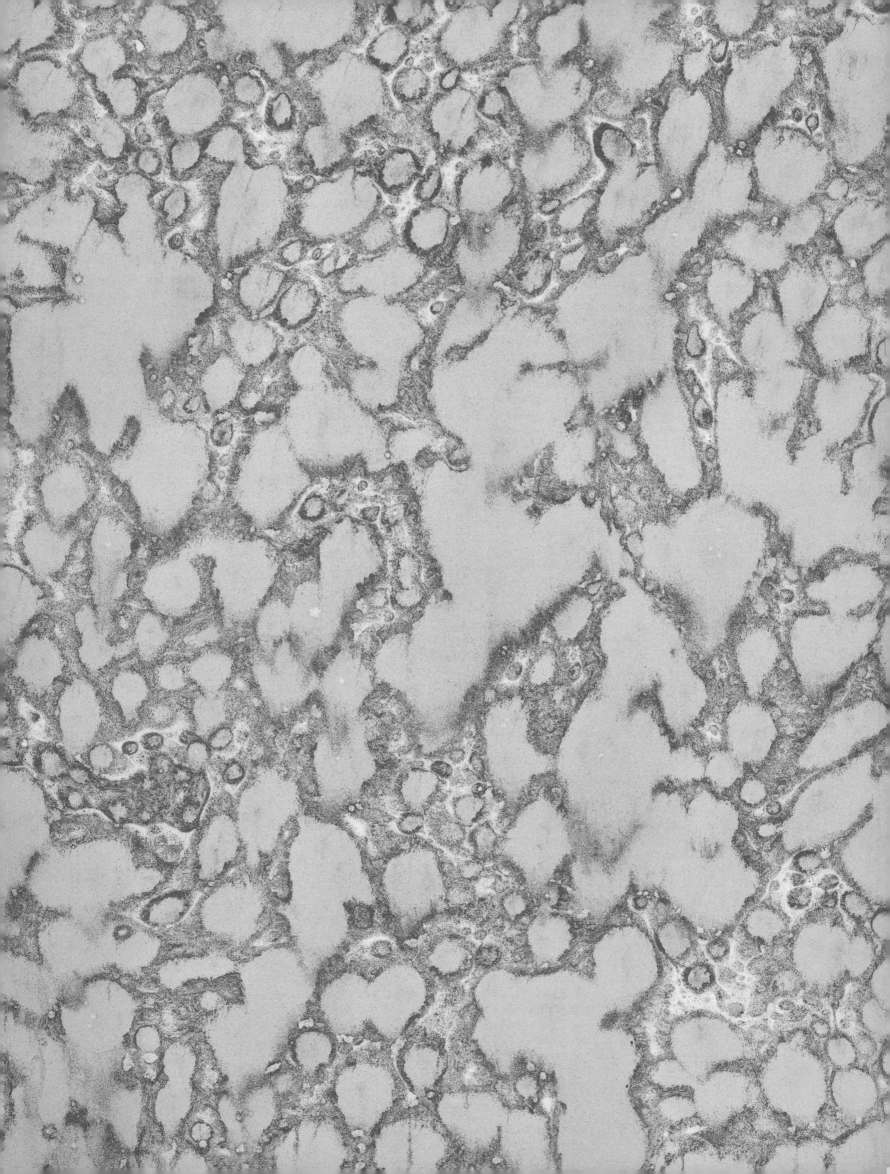